A GREAT FOOTBALL PROFESSIONAL —who went from college stardom to a long career as a pro football player—tells all about his craft.

Few know it as Earl Morrall does. He has been voted Most Valuable Player by the Detroit Lions, and the New York Giants; he led the Colts to victory after victory in their most memorable season, and was named Pro Football's Player of the Year.

He's been up, he's been down. Here is his story, **and** the inside story of the game and the people who play it!

The Earl Morrall Story
COMEBACK QUARTERBACK

By Earl Morrall and George Sullivan

GROSSET & DUNLAP
A NATIONAL GENERAL COMPANY
Publishers   New York

To my wife Jane and our children for their patience and understanding throughout my much-traveled career.

E.M.

ACKNOWLEDGMENTS

The authors wish to express their thanks to Dave Oliphant, Academic Book Service, Inc., West Haven, Connecticut, for his help in launching this project and to Don Weiss, Director of Public Relations, and Jim Heffernan, Director of Information, National Football League.

The Earl Morrall Story
COMEBACK QUARTERBACK

CHAPTER ONE

I spent my rookie year in professional football with the San Francisco Forty-Niners. I was twenty-two. They had Y. A. Tittle as their No. 1 quarterback. He was greatly skilled and beginning his ninth season as a pro, and he had probably forgotten much more football than I knew at the time.

But I wasn't awed by Tittle or any of the other players and it was no great problem for me to learn the formations and plays. From the day I arrived at training camp, I felt I could play in the National Football League, and it irked me that I had to wait until the sixth game of the season before Coach Frankie Albert gave me a starting assignment. I guess I had this attitude because playing football was just as natural for me as eating morning cornflakes.

I was born on May 17, 1934, in Muskegon, Michigan, and I began playing sports not long after I was out of the Pablum stage. That may be an exaggeration, but it's not a serious one. My brothers—Eddie, a year older, and Clarence, three years older—were sports-minded youngsters and they had me throwing a football, swinging a bat and shooting baskets as soon as I was capable.

My grandparents were of English stock. My father's family came from Shelby, Michigan, and moved to Muskegon in the early 1930's and opened a meat market. Our name is pronounced MORE-al; it rhymes with quarrel. My mother's parents—their name was Spencer—were from Baldwin, Michigan. They had a farm there.

My father was a good athlete and I guess my brothers

and I inherited our skills from him. He played semi-pro baseball and softball in Muskegon and he was also a talented golfer and bowler.

From the time I was five until my senior year in high school, we rented the first floor of a two-story wood frame house on Irwin Street. You could walk in almost any direction from that house and come to a playing field. Right across the street was a grade school and an open grassy area that was used as a football field, although the word "field," in this case, is something of a euphemism. The best that you could say for it was that it was flat. It was vaguely rectangular in shape, with the out-of-bounds lines formed by a cement sidewalk on one side and a row of prickly bushes on the other. A sprinkler connection jutted up from the ground at one end, a huge oak tree was at the other, while a steel flag pole was firmly rooted at about midfield. Even if there were no tacklers bearing down, you still had to do some pretty fancy broken field running.

Despite the hazards, we seldom played "touch"; we much preferred tackle. Eddie and I each had a pair of shoulder pads that Mother had bought each of us at an end-of-the-season sale one year for $3 each, but we had little else in the way of equipment.

When it began to grow dark and we couldn't see the ball well enough to play an organized game, we'd switch to Rough and Tumble. The rules were simple. Someone would throw the ball high into the air and whoever caught it became a marked man, pursued by all the others until he gave up the ball or it was taken from him. Then the new man was chased, and so it went, with boys dropping out one by one through exhaustion or the thought of waiting suppers. I remember those days well. There was something wonderfully fulfilling about them—the friendships, even the weariness.

Not only did we play football whenever we could, but we attended most of the high school team's home games, and two or three times a year, my father would pile all of us into the family automobile and take us to the out-of-town games, to Grand Haven, or Benton Harbor or Battle Creek. Then on the way home we'd discuss the games down to the most minute details—strategy, situations, and players' skills.

Part of the field across the street from our house was given over to a hard-packed clay court with a hoop and a backboard. I spent a good part of my boyhood days shooting baskets, and Eddie and I played two-on-two games with neighborhood friends. Later I played in a grade school basketball league. My school didn't have the facilities for the game so we had to use another school's gym. The basket was a hoop mounted on a post and planted in a heavy steel base that was rolled out to the center of the gym floor. It had no backboard and even layup shots had to be looped in.

Muskegon Central High School was a few blocks to the west and it offered a baseball diamond and a football field, but usually these facilities were reserved for the high school students and off limits to the neighborhood youngsters. McCrea Field, built in the late 1930's as a WPA project (my father worked on it), was a short bicycle ride in the opposite direction. We played a lot of baseball at McCrea.

If we didn't have enough players for full teams, we sometimes played Indian Ball. It required only four boys, two on a side, a pitcher and an outfielder. The field was a scaled-down version of a baseball diamond, with stakes close to the pitcher indicating the foul lines. We used the

9

chain link fence of a tennis court as a backstop. Each side had three outs, but there were no balls or strikes. The pitcher merely tried to get the ball over the plate. The hitter tried to reach first base before the outfielder retrieved the ball and got it back to the pitcher. I played an awful lot of Indian Ball. If the sport had had a Major League, I'm sure I could have made it.

Then to the south of our home was Marsh Field, with its rows of tiered wooden benches sheltered by rickety stands and the whole thing surrounded by a tall board fence, the type of ballpark that every American town of any size used to have. It was built in 1914. The Detroit Tigers backed a minor league team in Muskegon in 1940, but the league closed up shop when World War II began. Then in the late 1940's, when I was in my teens, Muskegon fielded a team in the Class A Central League. During the summer, the boys in the neighborhood made attending the games a nightly ritual. Of course, we never paid to get in. We'd lean our bikes against the fence, then stand on the seats and peer over the top. And there were tall trees near the park and you could climb one and seat yourself on a limb and watch. One hot summer night when I was thirteen or fourteen, the Detroit Lions played an intrasquad exhibition game at Marsh Field. Tickets cost $4, an unheard of price. All the kids took to the trees. Not long after the game started, the police came and chased us away. But when they left, we went right back up again.

During the baseball season another trick was to retrieve a foul ball which could be redeemed for an admission ticket. But usually when we recovered a ball, we'd keep it and use it in our own games. Eddie and I became extremely skilled as ball chasers, and foul tips supplied our needs for years. In fact, we became so accomplished that

10

eventually the club put us on their payroll, paying us a dollar a game to bring back anything sent out of the park, fair or foul.

In the early 1950's Muskegon's minor league team, like similar teams in every part of the country, drowned in a sea of red ink, and organized baseball probably ended for all time in the city. The old stands were torn down and the pine boards with their convenient knotholes were replaced by a sturdy chain link fence. You don't have to stand on a bicycle seat now. You can see right through, but no one bothers to watch. They're home in front of their television sets.

I never had a sports "idol" as a youngster, certainly not among the professional football players of my youth. After all, pro football was not nearly as popular in the years I was growing up as it is today. Games weren't nationally televised. The sport didn't become really popular until the late 1950's. When I was growing up, the biggest names I knew were college players, like Chuck Ortman and Pete Elliott at Michigan. There was also Everett (Sonny) Grandelius, a stocky power runner with sledge-hammer legs. He was a high school star at Muskegon Heights, then an All American at Michigan State and, in 1953, a leading ground gainer for the New York Giants. Later he became freshman coach and then backfield coach at Michigan State.

Bennie Oosterban was another athlete whose name I knew well. Bennie came earlier, however. An end who often caught passes one-handed and with either hand, Bennie was All State at Muskegon High in the early 1920's, and, later, a Walter Camp All American at Michigan. His greatest achievements were as Michigan's coach. He was "Coach of the Year" in 1948, his first season as head coach. In 1950,

11

when I was finishing up at junior high school, Bennie took Michigan to Pasadena and beat California in the Rose Bowl.

There was no one baseball player I admired more than any other. I was never a real fan of the game. The Detroit Tigers had some pretty good teams during the late 1940's —they won the World Series in 1945—and sometimes I'd listen to their games on the radio. I still feel that Harry Heilman was one of the best broadcasters of all time. But I never was overly enthusiastic about the club. To me, baseball wasn't a game you listened to or watched. It was a game you played. And during the spring and summer, I played every chance I got. The same with basketball and football in the fall.

Our family wasn't poverty stricken but we had to forgo a lot of things that are deemed necessities today, and there was never any money for luxury items. If I wanted a baseball glove or a new football, or even a pair of trousers, I went out and earned the money. My father worked intermittently. My mother worked. Housekeeping didn't interest her. She always had a job. When my brothers and I came home from school, the house would be empty. We'd eat something, change clothes, and go out and play.

I really didn't have any ambition to be a doctor, lawyer, or an engineer. I can't name a single profession that held any appeal for me. Sports were my chief interest. Indeed, aside from my school studies, virtually my only interest.

Later, when I was on high school teams, I never minded the long hours of practice. I never minded the fatigue. It didn't bother me that I hardly ever had a chance to sit around and do nothing, although I guess every person likes to be irresponsible once in a while. Some people might say I sacrificed a lot in order to play sports, or that I was

12

wholly dedicated to the idea. But I never thought of what I was doing in those terms.

Baseball, basketball, football—each was exciting, each was a challenge. Each was a chance to be somebody.

CHAPTER TWO

Michigan's Lower Peninsula is about the same shape as the back of your left hand. Put the fingers together; hold it in front of you. Detroit is located at the base of the thumb. Muskegon, a port city on Lake Michigan, is on the other side, at the base of the little finger.

While a New England community might be oriented toward manufacturing, or a Kansas town might be strictly a farm community, the people in my part of the country have always been recreation minded. The topography of the Muskegon area provides what the local Area Development Council calls a "veritable wonderland for the outdoorsman." Picknicking and boating are as popular as television. Rabbits, wildfowl, deer and even bear were once plentiful, and early saloon keepers used to load their boats to the gunwales with downed ducks and serve the meat as a featured dish on their free lunch counters. In the latter part of the last century, Muskegonites killed passenger pigeons by the thousands, netting or snaring the birds and then clubbing them to death.

Logging dams across local streams provided ponds for trout fishing. Smallmouth bass were once so numerous in Wolf Lake that it wasn't necessary to use a pole; you could net them. Fish hatcheries were established in the Muskegon area as early as the 1870's and streams were stocked with brook trout and California salmon. It's still no problem to hook a perch off the breakwater.

Muskegon also has a rich tradition when it comes to organized sport. Baseball in the area goes back almost to

14

the time of Abner Doubleday. As early as 1869, Muskegon had an organized team playing a regular schedule of games. The town first gained national prominence in football in the early 1900's when a high school teacher named Bob Zuppke was pressed into service as the coach of the football team because no one else would take the job. Zuppke, of course, went on to an illustrious career at the University of Illinois. Red Grange was one of his prodigies.

A brilliant innovator, Zuppke coached Muskegon High to winning seasons in 1906 and 1908. In 1906, the rules of football permitted the forward pass for the first time, and Zuppke promptly devised the spiral pass, which permitted the ball to be thrown farther and with great accuracy. While other teams were merely lobbing the ball, the Muskegon offense featured the long, arrow-straight throw.

In those days, high school players had no uniforms; they wore "old clothes." Zuppke changed this. He insisted that each player dye his sweat shirt and stockings a bright red, the school color. Each boy also had to buy his own pants and mothers were asked to quilt protection into them.

When Zuppke moved to Illinois, and his teams began to dazzle opponents with their fancy strategy, Muskegonites just shrugged. They had seen it all before from the wooden bleachers at Hackley Field.

Muskegon's eminence did not wane after Zuppke left. In 1912, Coach Louis Gudelsky produced a remarkable team. They defeated Hastings, 216–0, and the very next game turned back Ferris Institute, 137–0. But on Thanksgiving Day that year they lost the state title to Grand Rapids, 14–13. Grand Rapids *really* must have had a powerhouse.

In a winning streak that began in 1925, Coach Leo

Redmond steered the Muskegon team through thirty-seven games without a loss. There were two ties. Beginning in 1936, still under Redmond, the team piled up twenty-eight victories without a loss. When Redmond resigned in 1946, Harry Potter took over. Potter was the coach when I arrived at Muskegon High in the fall of 1948.

In ninth grade, my last year in junior high school, I played fullback. We used the single wing so I got to throw once in a while. I expected to be a fullback in high school, but one summer afternoon before my sophomore year, Potter said he was making me the quarterback on the varsity team. "The job is yours," he said. "It's yours for three years." Just like that.

I'm sure my height was one factor in Potter's decision. After ninth grade, I had really sprouted up, and I was close to six feet tall during my freshman year in high school, three or four inches taller than most of the boys my age. Someone once remarked that in a baseball uniform I looked like Ted Williams. I may have, but not when I went up to hit.

Potter also knew that I had played a good deal of basketball, a sport that requires plenty of coordination. I guess he figured whatever football I didn't know he could teach me. Another factor was that I was an honor student in my studies. Potter knew there would be no danger of my flunking out.

We operated out of the T and I felt awkward at first because the quarterback position was so new to me. I was also uncomfortable because my teammates were at least a year or two older than I was. But Potter constantly encouraged me.

He never stopped trying to get the guys to improve. "There's no perfect player," he told us more than once.

16

Football is a "habit game," he believed. The way to achieve success, he said, was to learn the game's fundamentals so thoroughly that you got so you could execute them almost instinctively.

Once I become a sophomore in high school, sports became a year 'round routine. It began with football in the fall, followed by basketball in the winter, then baseball in the spring. During the week or two respite between seasons, I remember how strange it was not to have to practice and be able to come home in the afternoon. And when I went to and from school, I remember always having a rolled-up towel tucked under my arm. Muskegon High, like most schools of the day, had no laundry service for the athletes.

In basketball, I was a forward. In my sophomore year the team went to the state playoffs and I was named to the third team by the All State selectors. But this was my zenith as far as my attainments in basketball were concerned. When I went to college, I concentrated on football and baseball. Basketball, in addition to the engineering course I took, would have been too much.

I liked baseball more than any other sport. I was a third baseman. I played in pick-up games; I played American Legion ball during the summer; and I played for my high school team. We won the state finals during my senior year and I was named All State.

Besides my involvement with sports, I had a newspaper route. It covered six miles. I delivered the Grand Rapids *Herald*, a morning paper. I'd get up at 5:30 A.M., and pedal my bike around the route. It took an hour and a half, longer in the winter when there was snow on the ground and I'd have to walk. Then I'd have breakfast and go to school. After school, there was always practice. And

17

after practice, I'd come home, have dinner, and then study. My older brother was a good student, always on the honor roll. He set an example that Eddie and I tried to follow. Sure, I had a long day. But I never really minded it.

Coach Potter had a short temper and gave out some memorable tongue lashings. But he had the utmost confidence in me and I'm sure this was a significant factor in the success I achieved in high school. For one thing, he never questioned my play-calling. Once in a game against Benton Harbor, we had the ball on our four-yard line. "Never pass in your own territory" was an axiom that quarterbacks followed in those days, at least high school quarterbacks did. Well, I called a pass play and I had to go back into my own end zone to get the ball away. The pass went incomplete, and when I came off the field, Potter didn't say a word. Even if the play had backfired, I don't think he would have been upset with me. Knowing that he had this kind of confidence in me helped me a great deal.

I was also the team's kicker, punting the ball and booting placements.

We had outstanding teams in 1949 and 1950, but in critical games we lost to Muskegon Heights, our chief rival. In 1951, my senior year, we hoped it would be different. We went through the season without losing once and then met the Heights in the final game. The two towns just about shut down for the game. Hackley Field was jammed to the rafters and scalpers hawked tickets like it was the Super Bowl or something. In the first half I set-up one touchdown with a twenty-five-yard run and passed for a second. I connected for two more touchdowns in the second half. We won, 26-6.

The game brought us the state interscholastic championship and newspaper recognition all the way to Detroit. Potter was being likened to Zuppke and I, a unanimous All State selection, was being compared to Sonny Grandelius and Bennie Oosterban. It was all quite unbelievable.

CHAPTER THREE

When I first entered high school, I never thought about going on to college. I knew my parents didn't have the money to send me. Besides, I really had no solid career ambitions, perhaps because the Korean War was being fought at the time and I figured my future was in the hands of the military. I planned to enter the Air Force.

In 1950 my attitude began to change. We had an excellent halfback on our high school team named Bruce Bosma and the University of Michigan was interested in him. They invited him to come to the campus at Ann Arbor, about a two-and-a-half-hour drive from Muskegon, and he asked me to go along. What I saw there really impressed me.

The size of the operation was what struck me first. There were three campuses, not just one, with well over a hundred buildings. It looked like the grounds could have held all of Muskegon. One campus was called the Athletic Campus. It included the huge football stadium, the baseball field and other athletic fields, a golf course, an intramural sports building, a swimming pool—everything.

It was another world for me. After that trip I made up my mind I would go to college, if not to Michigan, then someplace else. As for the money necessary, I figured I'd work my way through. My oldest brother was doing that. It didn't occur to me that I might be awarded an athletic scholarship. I never looked upon football as a means of furthering my education. I'm always amazed when I speak to high school youngsters today and learn how carefully they have planned their lives, and how many of them look upon football or some other sport as a stepping stone to college and a career. I never did. I played football for the enjoyment and satisfaction I got from the sport; that's all.

I did well in my studies in high school, just as I had in junior high. Friday and Saturday nights were the only ones that Eddie and I didn't spend at least an hour or two on homework. It paid off. In my senior year I was named as a member of the National Honor Society of Secondary Schools.

It was early in my senior year that I first began to hear from college recruiters, and as our high school team continued to win game after game the number of persuaders that contacted me spiraled upward. I don't know exactly how many colleges I heard from, but there were at least a dozen that offered me full scholarships. A writer for the local paper once asked me if I was impressed by all the attention. "It's not really a question of being impressed," I told him. " 'Bewildered' is a better word." A year before I hadn't even been planning to go to college. Then suddenly some of the foremost universities in the country wanted and were willing to pay my way. No wonder I was a bit dazed.

Eventually I reduced the list to five—Purdue, Notre Dame, Dartmouth, Michigan, and Michigan State. Making the final decision was more difficult than any third and three situation I've ever faced. First of all, I simply didn't have the time to spend making a careful evaluation. After the football season, I swung right into basketball and I'd have to practice every afternoon. Then in the spring there was baseball. I studied evenings to keep my marks up and I worked weekends at a local clothing store. So I didn't have the time to visit campuses, meet coaches and all the rest.

Month after month went by and the pressure mounted. People I'd meet in the street never failed to ask me, "What school are you going to?" The local newspaper, the Muskegon *Chronicle*, wanted to know. And the colleges themselves pressed me with telephone calls and letters.

I simply didn't want to make a mistake. I realized that I was going to give up four years of my life and I didn't want them to be wasted years. Unfortunately, I didn't have anyone I could go to for advice. "I can't tell you what to do," my father had told me. "I never went to college; I don't know which ones are right for you and which aren't." The people who were in a position to advise me were all alumni of one college or another. In other words, each was biased.

When I graduated from high school in June 1952, I still hadn't made up my mind although I had narrowed down the choice to either Michigan or Michigan State.

Unless you know the state of Michigan and its people, it's difficult to appreciate the intense rivalry that exists between the two schools. This story may illustrate. In the summer after I graduated from high school, I took a job at Smitty's Beverage Company in Muskegon, loading cases of soda and beer on delivery trucks. The company was owned by John (Smitty) Vanderplow, a Michigan State alumnus. Not long after I started work, Michigan supporters charged that I was being "influenced." One story had it that I had been put on Vanderplow's payroll at $150 a week. Another claim was that Vanderplow had given me a new car to use. Both rumors were bandied about in newspapers all over the state, and they eventually reached the ears of Kenneth (Tug) Wilson, the Big Ten Commissioner, who, until he investigated, gave them some credence. It was quite a furor.

Another time, the Muskegon *Chronicle,* whose management was University of Michigan oriented, announced flatly that I had selected Michigan over Michigan State. I hadn't. I hadn't even discussed the subject with them. I believe they were trying to pressure me into choosing Michigan.

Many people I spoke to downgraded Michigan State. I was told that I'd be sure to get a better education at Michigan, that State was fine if you wanted to be a veterinarian or a meat inspector. And because it was a landgrant school, some people referred to it as a "cow college" or called it "Moo U."

Looking back, I realize that what tipped the scales in favor of Michigan State was a visit I made to the campus in East Lansing during March of my senior year in high school. First of all, I was impressed by its size. It is a huge and modern educational plant.

At the athletic office, there was a warm and friendly relationship between the coaches and the players. People were on a first name basis. Biggie Munn was then the coach and I had a nice chat with him. "Earl," he said, "you'll get a chance to throw the football here."

Then later Munn told me that he felt I could become an All American at Michigan State. But this didn't impress me nearly as much as the over-all feeling I came away with that Munn and the other coaches really wanted me.

Previously I had visited the Michigan campus. I really didn't have what you would call a meeting with Bennie Oosterban, then the coach. It was more of an audience. I remember it clearly. He had a huge desk and I sat across from him. He put a cigar in his mouth, leaned way back

23

in his swivel chair and swung his feet up. I was looking into the soles of his shoes, and I felt like I was about to be interviewed for a job stoking furnaces or waiting on table.

In August I finally decided upon Michigan State. I called Biggie Munn.

"Fine," he said. "You'll like it here. You won't ever regret it." I never have.

CHAPTER FOUR

Michigan State used what was known as a "multiple offense." As quarterback, I was always moving backs or flanking guys. I ran with the ball, blocked and got to throw. It was great schooling.

We set-up like this:

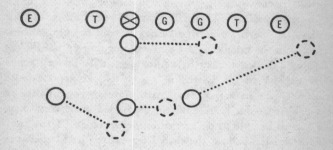

I was stationed behind the center, just as in the conventional T. The fullback was about five yards directly in back of me with halfbacks on either side, a step or two ahead. I could take the snap from center as any T quarterback does, or the ball could be centered through my legs to the fullback, just as if he were the tailback in the single wing. Or we could shift into a conventional single wing and then run our play.

The system was the doing of Clarence L. (Biggie) Munn, an all-time great guard from Minnesota who came to Michigan State as a coach in 1947. Biggie had served under people like Bernie Bierman, Ozzie Solem, and Fritz Crisler, and he knew as much about football as there was to know. He coached a year at Syracuse and while there he hired a former Syracuse guard named Hugh (Duffy) Daugherty as assistant coach. When Biggie signed with Michigan State, he brought Duffy with him. Duffy was his line coach for seven years. Then in 1953, when Munn became State's athletic director, Daugherty took over as head coach.

Much of my football knowledge came from these two great coaches. Once a game got underway, they left things pretty much in my hands. They would send in three or four plays, no more. I'd give ball-carrying and blocking assignments in the huddle. If a team was clogging up the middle on us, I'd spread them by calling a split T. I'd call single wing plays to get a back in a good blocking position or to put him in a spot for a pass, just as you might use a flanker in the T. The system demanded great versatility. I had to be able to do everything, even block. If the full-back got the ball on the snap from center, he'd often spin and hand to the halfback, in which case I had to lead the interference.

We also worked belly-series plays. I'd get the ball on a direct snap from center, then turn and "ride" the full-back—put the ball in his belly and take a step with him into the line. I'd either let him keep the ball or I'd fake and hand to the halfback. Or I could keep it myself, roll to the right, and shoot a pass.

I played safety on defense and I was also the team's punter. We quick-kicked a number of times. It would be third down and we'd be deep in our own territory, then I'd boot one. Sometimes the next play would be run off from the opposition's five or ten yard line. It was beautiful.

Sometimes we faked the quick-kick, working a reverse with a handoff to halfback.

When everything was working right, the opposition never knew what was coming next. Terry Brennan, then Notre Dame's coach, said the multiple offense was impossible to figure out. I'm sure there were many other coaches who agreed with him.

Limited substitution came in during my sophomore year and the two platoon system was out. This worked to the advantage of second-team players like myself since it gave us a much greater opportunity to play than we might have had otherwise. Once a substitute was sent into the game, he had to remain in until two minutes before the quarter ended.

Even though I was deeply involved with football during my stay at Michigan State, I still played a lot of baseball. During my sophomore year, I was the second string third baseman on the varsity team and we were good enough to take part in the College World Series in Omaha, but we were eliminated in an early round. As a junior I played on the varsity and batted .312, and the next year I switched to shortstop.

During the summer, I played baseball for a team in the Iowa State League, a league made up of college players. I played for Spencer, a farm town in the northwestern corner of the state. All the games were played at night. During the day we held down jobs in town, and mine was installing television antennas for an electrical supply company.

Switching back and forth from football to baseball did present some problems. When you throw a baseball, you break your wrist. But in football you throw stiff-wristed.

Tom Yewcic was first-string quarterback during my

sophomore year. He was injured in the Iowa game and the following week Biggie started me against Minnesota. Everything went great and we won, 21–20. But the next week Yewcic was back. He led the team to an undefeated season and a win in the Rose Bowl over UCLA. He also earned himself All American honors and a job with the Boston Patriots in the American Football League.

Then Yewcic graduated, along with two other members of the starting backfield. As a junior I started every game, but I'm sure there were many days that Daugherty, who had replaced Munn by this time, wished he had Yewcic back. Newspapers often used the word "dismal" to describe the season and that's just what it was. We finished with a 3–6 record, the worst for Michigan State since 1919.

It's difficult to say why the 1954 season contrasted so sharply with the one that preceded it. There may have been some overconfidence, a tendency on the part of some of the team's veterans to rest upon the laurels they had won in Pasadena the year before. However, I don't think we were quite so bad as our won-lost record would indicate. We gained more than 400 yards against Notre Dame and another 400 against Purdue, but in each case we were beaten. And there were a couple of games we lost by only a point or two.

At the beginning of the 1955 football season, I doubt if it would have surprised many people if Duffy had announced that I was being relegated to the bench. What had happened the year before was still fresh in everyone's mind and I was probably identified with the team's failure more closely than anyone else. In addition, I missed the team's spring drills because I was involved with baseball. Spring practice at State is highlighted by the annual Green-White game, the varsity facing alumni players, and a pair of sophomores, Jim Ninowski and Pat Wilson, shared the quarterbacking for the varsity, and they did so well that they were named co-winners of the game's most valuable player trophy. More than one person figured my football career might have seen its best days. But I went out and won my job back and it turned out to be a great year. In fact, I couldn't have scripted it better.

The season didn't start out in stirring fashion, however. We barely got by Indiana in our opening game, 20–13. The following week we went to Ann Arbor to meet Michigan, then rated the No. 2 team in the nation and heavily favored to win the Big Ten title. We outrushed them, outpassed them, and outpunted them, but a blocked kick, an interception and some fumbles killed us. Only twice did they cross into our territory but they scored both times. We lost, 14–7. But I've often thought that game helped to make us a better team. We came out of it with great determination. The next week we rebounded against Stanford, a game in which I scored my first college touchdown. Notre Dame was next.

I didn't realize it at the time, but I think I may have made All American and started myself on the way to my career in pro football the day we played the Fighting Irish. They came into East Lansing with an eleven-game winning streak. In beating SMU, Indiana, and Miami that season, they hadn't even been scored upon. All the polls had them rated No. 1 in the country.

We scored first. Late in the first quarter I hit Clarence Peaks with a pass good for twenty-two yards and a first down on the Notre Dame 21. I followed with a twelve-yard run that got us a first down on the 9. Two plays later Peaks knifed into the end zone. Notre Dame tied the score in the second quarter on a pass from Paul Hornung to Jim Morse, a play that covered forty yards.

We kicked off to begin the second half, but the Irish couldn't move the ball and punted. Then we took over on our own 20 yard line and in nine plays we were in their end zone, Gerry Planutis going over from the one. I scored our third touchdown. Planutis recovered a Notre Dame fumble on the Irish 16. Bootlegging the ball, I got to the Notre Dame one and just missed going in. I kept the ball again on the next play, hit the line, rolled to the right and over the goal line. That was it; we won, 21–7.

"When you beat Notre Dame, you're in the big leagues," Duffy said after. Indeed, it was an important game, but it was especially significant because it was carried on network television. An estimated fifty million people saw it.

Hornung had a fine game and if it weren't for some untimely penalty calls, the outcome might have been different. Jim Morse, the Notre Dame left halfback, was another star that day. Morse and I had been boyhood chums. He was twice All State at St. Mary's High in Muskegon at the same time I was quarterbacking Muskegon High, but this was the first time we had ever met on the football field.

Our team never lost momentum after beating Notre Dame.

We handled Illinois and Wisconsin without too much trouble. In the Purdue game the following week. I intercepted one of Len Dawson's laterals and took off on a ninety-yard touchdown run. We won that one, 20–0. In the dressing room after the game, we heard the news that Illinois had upset Michigan, dropping them into a tie with us in conference standings. A Rose Bowl trip now loomed as a distinct possibility. Undefeated Ohio State led the conference standings, but the Buckeyes, having represented the Big Ten at Pasadena the previous season, were not eligible this time.

We finished up by beating Minnesota and Marquette, and on the last Saturday of the season Ohio State did us the favor of knocking off Michigan, 17–0. The following Monday the Big Ten athletic directors formerly certified us the conference Rose Bowl Representatives.

I had made the trip to Pasadena with the team in 1954, but I was a sophomore at the time, second string behind Yewcic, and although I played in the game, I didn't make much of a contribution. This time my status was far different. It was a carnival—celebrities, interviews, speeches, parades, and a sunburn in December. About 4,500 Michigan State students made the trip to Pasadena, with 2,600 of them traveling in six special trains. Someone said it was the largest non-military migration ever to head West from a single point.

And I have a special reason for remembering the Rose Bowl. While I was playing baseball for Spencer, Iowa, in the summer of 1954, I met an Iowa University coed from Washington, Iowa, named Jane Whitehead. She was working at Clear Lake, a resort area, during the summer, teaching water skiing during the day and waiting on table evenings. We became engaged during the Rose Bowl festivities and she became Jane Morrall in June that year.

Our Rose Bowl opposition was UCLA, a team similar to ours in a number of ways. They had a versatile, well-balanced attack and a quick defensive line, but whereas we used the multiple offense, UCLA was strictly a single wing club.

Two plays stand out in my memory—our first play from scrimmage and our last one. We won the toss and elected to receive. Walt Kowalcyzk, our halfback, brought the ball out to the 12. On first down I called a belly-series pass, a play the coaches had put in to take UCLA by surprise. I was to take the snap from center, fake to the fullback, fake to the halfback, then roll to the right. Dave Kaiser, our sophomore right end, was to run a down and out, while Walt Kowalcyzk was to slip out on the flat, and either one of them was to be my target.

As I set-up to throw, I could see both men were in the clear. I could go either long or short; I decided to go short. I knew exactly where I had to put the ball. Then came one of those fatal slips between intent and execution. I tightened up or something. I don't know. But the ball wobbled drunkenly in the air, then nosed down. Jim Decker, the UCLA cornerback, and the man who had been faked out, merely leaned back—he didn't even have to leap—and made the interception. He was brought down on our 16 yard line. The Bruins quickly scored from there.

That's how the Rose Bowl game started.

We tied up the game on a touchdown that Walt Kowalcyzk set up with a thirty-yard run off tackle that put the ball on the UCLA 17 yard line. Two plays later I hit Clarence Peaks with a pass in the end zone. And early in the fourth quarter we went ahead when I pitched out to Peaks who fired a pass to end John Lewis on the 20. Lewis broke away from a UCLA safety to score. We couldn't hold the Bruins, however, and they scored again, making 14–14 as we went into the final minutes.

It had a storybook finish.

We had the ball. With Peaks and Gerry Planutis doing the carrying, we were driving for their end zone. We tried a field goal from their 24. Planutis booted but it was short. On first down on their own 20, UCLA was hit with an unsportsmanlike conduct penalty that set them back to their five. Ronnie Knox tried to pass from his own end zone, but our defense poured in on him. He threw in desperation and the officials called him for intentionally grounding the ball, penalizing UCLA half the distance to the goal line.

Now the Bruins punted, and Clarence Peaks called for a fair catch at about midfield, but just as he was about to gather in the ball, a UCLA player slammed into him. This cost them another fifteen yards, putting the ball on the UCLA 35. An eleven-yard pass play brought the ball to their 24. There were only seven seconds left. A field goal was the only call.

I decided I wanted Dave Kaiser to kick. He wasn't our regular kicker but he had looked terrific in practice during the week. Duffy had called a time out and I sprinted to the sidelines to tell him I wanted Kaiser, but he had the very same idea. "Put Kaiser back to kick," he was screaming.

I held the ball. Dave booted. It was beautiful, perfect all the way, clearing the crossbar by four or five feet.

Many people, when you mention the 1956 Rose Bowl, remember Kaiser's kick. I remember it, too, but I also have a haunting memory of that first pass play and the years haven't dimmed it any.

Toward the end of the season, a flood of All American teams had been announced. In the mid-1950's, two of the most publicized were the teams selected by *Collier's* and *Look*. The *Collier's* squad was chosen by the Football Coaches Association, and the *Look* team by the Football Writers Association of America. I was named quarterback on both. The competition included Paul Hornung, George

Welsh of Navy, Len Dawson of Purdue, and Fred Wyant of West Virginia. Hornung had come off with a clear-cut decision over Welsh when Notre Dame downed Navy, and the fact that we had turned back Notre Dame helped to give me the edge over Hornung. I was also named to All American teams selected by the Associated Press, International News Service, *The Sporting News, NBC-TV* and *CBS-TV.*

With 1,047 yards gained rushing and passing, I was seventh among the nation's offense leaders. I had completed twenty-five passes out of thirty-nine, a .641 percentage. I had punted fourteen times, averaging 48.7 yards per kick. Only one kicker did better than that, Don Chandler of Florida who later became a punting star at Green Bay and New York.

Naturally, with this kind of a record, the pros were very interested in me. But I didn't know whether I was interested in them. Nowadays whenever I go to a banquet or some other type of public affair, someone is sure to grab me and say, "Earl, look at this boy. He's got good size; he's got good speed. He's got a great chance of making it in the pros." Then I'll talk to the youngster and find out he's only a high school senior or a college freshman. This always surprises me. It was very different in my time. Pro salaries then were nothing to get very excited about. A good many players were receiving no more than $6,500 or $7,000. I was planning a career in engineering and I knew that beginning engineers were earning that much. Even the biggest "name" players of the day—Bobby Layne, Otto Graham, and Norm Van Brocklin—weren't getting much more than $20,000. I could never say that becoming a pro football player was one of my prime ambitions, and it wasn't until my senior year at Michigan State that I even began to consider a pro career as a possibility.

My first real contact with pro ball came in the form of a telegram. It was dated November 29, 1955. It read:

> HAPPY TO INFORM YOU THAT YOU WERE OUR FIRST DRAFT CHOICE. OUR HEAD COACH RED STRADER HAS SPOKEN TO COACH DAUGHERTY AND I WILL CONTACT YOU BY PHONE. BEST OF LUCK IN THE ROSE BOWL.

It was signed, "Lou Spadia, General Manager, San Francisco Forty-Niners."

CHAPTER FIVE

The day after the Rose Bowl game I met with Spadia and Frankie Albert, the Forty-Niners' coach (Red Strader had been fired), to discuss contract terms. They offered me a salary of $11,000, plus a $1,000 bonus. Sonny Grandelius, the Michigan State backfield coach at the time, had been advising me and I asked Spadia if he could join the meeting. He gave me a non-committal shrug.

I went and got Sonny and after the introductions, Spadia said, "We've offered Earl a real fine contract, Sonny—a $12,000 salary, plus a $1,000 bonus."

At first I thought I didn't hear right. Then it hit me. Sonny's presence had caused them to jump the price by a thousand dollars. The value of negotiation could not have been made more clearer to me.

We talked some more but the figures remained about the same. Canadian football was the only leverage a college player had in those days. Both Ottawa and Saskatchewan had made me offers, but I wasn't too interested. I wanted the NFL. I guess Spadia and Albert realized this.

Then I explained I didn't want to sign right away, that I wanted to be able to play baseball at Michigan State in the spring, and if I signed I'd lose my amateur standing. This was true. I was looking forward to baseball. It would have been a miserable spring if I was made to sit out the season.

When baseball ended, Spadia visited me at Michigan State. One night, he, Grandelius and I talked until dawn. We managed to get the salary boosted to $14,000, with a $2,000 bonus, although Spadia had to call Tony Morabito, the Forty-Niners' owner, to get his authorization to go that high. Times sure have changed. At any rate, that's the figure I signed for.

Late in July I had a few briefing sessions with the Forty-Niners' coaches, but then I had to report to the training camp of the College All Americans in Chicago to prepare for the All Star Game. I was to be the starting quarterback. Curly Lambeau was the coach. We were playing the Cleveland Browns.

I worked hard in the practice sessions and, along with center Bob Pellegrini from Maryland, was named the team's co-captain. Early in the game on a first down play, I pitched out to Lenny Moore. That's about all I remember. Someone clobbered me and the next thing I knew I was lying on the ground in back of the bench and the team doctor was asking me, "What's the score." I didn't know. Then he asked me to name some of our plays. I gave him plays, but they were ones we had used at Michigan State. It wasn't until after half-time that my brain began to function right. The All Stars lost, 26–0. "Disastrous" Lambeau called it. "Painful" was the word I used.

I had some misgivings about going to the Forty-Niners training camp. Having lived in Michigan, I had heard stories of how Bobby Layne, the Lions' quarterback, had harassed young rookies unmercifully. But it wasn't like that at San Francisco. Rookie hazing was kept to a minimum, and Y. A. Tittle, the Forty-Niners' No. 1 quarterback, kind of took me under his wing.

"The pro game is throwing," Tittle told me the first week I was in camp. "Put the ball in the air; that's the way to win." I had passed in college, of course, but often merely to keep the defenses honest. Here there was no pre-

37

tense about it. And there were more receivers and every one of them was skilled. I would throw for hour after hour to Gordie Soltau, Billy Wilson, Bill Jessup, and Clyde Connor and they never seemed to tire. They ran pattern after pattern—in, out and back, and long and short. It was great training but at night my arm had a throbbing ache like it never had before.

We had three of the greatest ball carriers ever to play in the same backfield—Joe Perry, Hugh McElhenny and John Henry Johnson. They were often called the "Million Dollar Backfield." When I arrived upon the scene, however, the price tag had been marked down because of age and injury. We also had Leo Nomellini, a wrestler who had become an All League linebacker, and Bob St. Clair, a tackle and the biggest man I had ever seen. He stood 6-foot-9; he weighed 270. And he ate raw meat. It wasn't a put-on; he really enjoyed it. I remember going to a restaurant with him once and the waiter saying, "How would you like your steak done, sir?"

"Raw," Bob answered.

"Raw?"

"Yeah, raw."

"You mean very rare, sir?"

"No, I mean raw."

The waiter couldn't bring himself to believe what he heard. When he brought the steak, it had been browned on each side, just touched to a frying pan.

"Take it back," Bob ordered. "When I saw raw, I mean raw. Not even warm."

A few minutes later the waiter returned with a cold, raw steak. Bob ate heartily.

St. Clair's eccentric eating habits were well known to everyone. Once I invited him to the house and Jane asked

38

him to stay for lunch. Jane was a bit awed by him; first, because of his size, and, second, because he was a veteran player. She didn't know whether to serve his hot dog raw or cooked. Timidly, she asked.

"It doesn't matter," he said. "Just cook it along with the others."

Jane thought he was awfully gracious.

The Forty-Niners had had a disasterous season the year before, losing eight of twelve games which put them next to last in the Western Conference standings. Strader was then let go and Frankie Albert, who had quarterbacked Stanford in the Rose Bowl game of 1941, took over. Relaxed and easy-going, Albert had been the Forty-Niners' quarterback for six years, but as a coach his experience was limited to a year as an assistant to Strader. Albert named Howard (Red) Hickey, another of Strader's assistants, as his backfield coach and gave him a wide range of other responsibilities.

Hickey had come under the influence of Paul Brown, the amazingly successful head coach of the Cleveland Browns; in fact, Hickey seemed to have been mesmerized by him. Like Brown, he wanted everything exact. "On this pattern," he'd tell an end, "run three steps down and five steps out." And he meant three steps and five steps, no more, no less. And when he told an end to split six yards from the tackle, he wanted him to split precisely six yards, not five or seven.

And Hickey called the plays, just as Paul Brown did. Clyde Connor and Gordie Soltau, two ends, were used alternately to bring them in. The team would huddle, then either Connor or Soltau would appear and announce: "Hickey says to run a forty-five trap." Then the quarterback would say, "Forty-five trap."

This worked well when Otto Graham was quarterbacking the Cleveland Browns, but it has never worked with success anywhere else. Even Graham resented the system and when he took over as head coach of the Washington Redskins, he let Sonny Jurgensen, his quarterback, run the ball game.

I accepted the situation. After all, I was a rookie. But with Tittle it was different. Sideline quarterbacking infuriated him. He felt the quarterback had to be the one who controlled the game, constantly probing and analyzing defenses to set-up the opposition for the kill. He felt the Hickey system robbed him of his tactical skill, that he was nothing but a puppet.

Tittle's frustration built and his play began to show it. Eventually there were some sharp words between Albert and Y. A. But the coach would not back down.

"I'm the coach," he told Tittle, "and I'll call the plays and you'll do what I tell you. If you don't want to go along, maybe we'll make some changes."

Y. A. went along, but he still didn't like it. The team won its first three exhibition games, lost the next three, and dropped the season's opener to the Giants. Mid-season approached and we had won only once. Then suddenly Albert did a turnabout. He announced that plays were no longer to be sent in from the bench. The quarterback was to run the game. And I was to be the quarterback!

I had split games with Tittle but this was my first starting assignment and I remember it as clearly as I do the 1969 Super Bowl game. We faced the Detroit Lions in Kezar Stadium before a near capacity crowd. The weather was perfect.

Detroit scored first, putting together a long touchdown drive in the second quarter that featured the running of

250-pound Leon Hart. The crowd oohed and aahed as he slammed holes in our line, finally blasting over from the three. On the kickoff that followed, Joe Arenas caught the ball on the 10, faked to his right, then scampered left. He was in the open before he reached midfield. Two Lions gave chase and were about to pounce on him when Charlie Powell threw a block clearing the way and Arenas made the end zone.

Both teams got field goals later in the period, making it 10–10 at halftime. In the third period, Hart scored another touchdown for the Lions and Gordie Soltau booted a field goal for us. It remained that way until the closing minutes. With 2:56 to go, we got a first down on the Detroit two. I was sure we were going to win.

I handed to John Henry Johnson, who gained close to a hundred yards for the day, and Johnson plunged over right tackle, but the Detroit defense moved up under him, stopping him at the one. It still looked like a cinch touchdown. We huddled and the crowd was screaming, "Go! Go! Go!," and I could hardly make myself heard. I called Johnson again. He dove—and made it, tumbling from the stack of piled-up bodies into the end zone. But our right tackle, the man who was supposed to clear a path for Johnson, had moved out ahead of the snap. It cost us the touchdown and a five-yard penalty.

Now we were on the six. There was less than a minute left, but I still thought we'd make it. I pitched out to Johnson. Linebacker Gene Cronin shot the gap and Johnson lost seven yards.

We had one more chance, maybe two. I called a sweep option pass to the right, a hand off to Hugh McElhenny. Hugh was our biggest running threat. I figured if they pressured him, he could pass, but if they played back,

Hugh was a good enough brokenfield runner to carry it in.

I gave the ball to McElhenny and they went for him. Billy Wilson got open in the end zone. A quarterback would have fired a bullet to Wilson, but McElhenny tossed a floater and it hung lazily in the air. A Detroit back—I believe it was Yale Lary—made an easy pickoff.

So ended my debut in the National Football League. I remember it because we lost, and for one other reason. Late in the game as we were driving toward the Lions' goal, I went back to pass. I got the ball away without any trouble, but just as I unloaded I caught a glimpse of a Lion player bearing down upon me, his elbows high and menacing, like a pair of bludgeons. I ducked; he missed, one elbow grazing my shoulder. Behind me there was an official and he instantly flung his flag to the ground.

"I never hit him!" my attacker protested.

"If you had hit him," the official said, "we'd have had to pick up his head at the 50 yard line." Then he walked off the fifteen yards.

I thought the man who had stormed in on me was Bob Long, a linebacker for the Lions. Years later I went to work for Gar Wood Industries. My boss was the Sales Manager, Sherwin (Sonny) Gandee, a one-time defensive end for Detroit. One night at dinner Sonny told me he had been my assailant that afternoon at Kezar Stadium. We laughed about it then, but it was a good thing for him he waited almost five years to tell me.

The week following the Detroit game, we played Los Angeles and Tittle and I shared the quarterbacking. It was a calamitous afternoon. We didn't score a single touchdown and the Rams, who had lost five in a row, whipped us, 30–6. The loss dropped us into last place.

42

Morabito was furious after the game. He accused some of the players of not giving a damn. "They only want to come around on Monday for their checks," he said. He threatened trades that would "take the whole team apart." It may have been Morabito's outburst, or it may have been because Albert had given the game back to the quarterbacks, but for some reason the team began to win. We beat Green Bay the next week, then tied Philadelphia, and we ended the season with consecutive wins over Baltimore, Green Bay and Baltimore. We finished with a 5–6–1 record.

I played in every game and I was well satisfied with my performance. Then late in 1957 the Forty-Niners announced that quarterback John Brodie was their No. 1 draft choice. Brodie had just completed a splendid season at Stanford and, aside from his talent, appealed to the Forty-Niners as a gate attraction. Y. A. and I were concerned, and that's putting it mildly. Three quarterbacks were considered a luxury no team could afford and one of us was going to have to go, we figured. But Red Hickey assured us there was no cause to worry. "It's already been decided," he said, "we're planning on carrying three quarterbacks next year."

In January I returned to Michigan State to earn additional credits toward my degree. I had taken a reduced number of credit courses in the fall semester of my junior and senior years, and I didn't make up the credits in summer school. I received my degree—in engineering—in June.

The next fall we were no better than mediocre in our pre-season games, winning three and losing three. Tittle did most of the quarterbacking.

I leased an apartment in San Carlos, not far from training camp in Redwood City. Jane flew out about two weeks

43

before season opened, bringing with her our first child, Matt, who had been born in May. We went out and bought a crib, a playpen, a highchair—everything.

It was the Sunday morning after Jane's arrival. The apartment was in chaos. Curtains were not yet hung and cartons of our belongings were strewn about. Chuck Smith, a sophomore end with the Forty-Niners, and his wife had spent the night with us. We didn't have an extra bed so we took the mattress off ours, put it on the floor, and they slept on that. We slept on the box spring.

Shortly after noon, the telephone rang. It was Frankie Albert. "Red Hickey and I would like to stop over and see you," he said.

"Fine," I answered. "Come ahead."

I didn't have the slightest idea what they wanted. "I guess it's just a friendly visit," I told Jane.

"How nice," she said, "They probably want to see the baby and find out if we're getting settled all right." Then we both scurried around trying to get the place in order.

I could see when they arrived that it was no friendly visit. Something was up.

"We've worked out a trade," Albert said. "We're sending you to Pittsburgh."

Before I had a chance to react, Albert began a long recitation of why the trade was being made. He explained that they wanted to move Brodie into the No. 2 spot behind Tittle and that they felt he would help to boost the gate since he was a local hero. In addition, they were getting a veteran linebacker—Marv Matuszak—from Pittsburgh, and, as I well knew, the team needed linebacking help badly. They were also getting Pittsburgh's No. 1 draft choices in 1958 and 1959.

After they left, Jane and I began packing up what

44

hadn't yet been unpacked, and stowing everything in the car for the long drive East. I wasn't too downcast. I could understand why the trade was made, and I knew that Buddy Parker, the Pittsburgh coach, had a desperate need for a quarterback. As for Jane, she was philosophical about it. "That's football," she said. It was an expression I was going to hear an awful lot in the next dozen years.

CHAPTER SIX

Raymond (Buddy) Parker, the Steelers' coach, was a grim-faced and gloomy Texan who newspapers often called the "old pro." Indeed, he had been around awhile.

He joined the Detroit Lions in 1935 as a backfield coach and two years later went to the Chicago Cardinals where he became player-coach in 1943. He took charge of the Lions in 1951 and steered them to two NFL championships—in 1952 and 1953.

Parker left the Lions under circumstances that can be only called bizarre. Shortly before the 1957 pre-season schedule began, Buddy was a guest at a "Meet the Lions" banquet, an annual affair sponsored by the team's most enthusiastic boosters. Introduced as the "best coach in the league," Parker took the microphone to announce that he was in possession of "the worst team in training camp that I have ever seen."

"These players have gotten too big for me or something," he told the open-mouthed audience. "I'm getting out of Detroit football. And I'm getting out tonight."

With that, Parker strode from the banquet hall and out of Detroit football. Sixteen days later the Steelers signed him.

Impulsiveness and impatience—these were two of Parker's dominating traits. A loss, a poor showing by the team, was sure to be followed by a flurry of releases or trades or both. Working with young players, building from the ground up, this was not his style. Parker wanted a winner tomorrow and believed the best way to achieve this goal was to trade for tried and proven players. One year Buddy went to the draft meetings without any selection until the eighth round, having traded away his first seven choices.

Parker's impatience was apparent whenever we lost, and he would heap abuse upon the team and individual players. Players would hide to escape his tirades. When Buddy coached the Lions, the club had a mortal fear of losing on the West Coast because there was virtually no way a man could avoid Parker's blistering harangue on the flight back. He would stride up and down the aisle, a drink in one hand, a cigarette in the other, and he would single out those he felt responsible for the loss, assaulting each one with a stream of invective. It was brutal. Players today wouldn't stand for such treatment. Some men would slouch down in their seats and cover their heads with blankets, hoping they would somehow be rendered invisible. Others took to spending the trip in the john. If you are, say, six-foot-three and weigh 230, spending three or four hours in the cramped confines of an airplane john can be torture, but players judged it to be better than a Parker tongue-lashing.

Parker's stormy moods wore off quickly, however. When we turned out for practice the next day, he was a changed man—calm, soft-spoken, a regular prince.

You never knew about Buddy. I'd be on my way to the practice field and I'd see him and I'd say, "Hi, Buddy." He might answer with a cheery "Good morning," or with a dour nod, or sometimes he looked in the other direction. I never knew anyone so moody.

Pittsburgh's recent record had been awfully bleak. They had not had a winning season since 1949, a year they achieved (if that is the word) six wins against five losses.

Losing had gotten to be accepted as a matter of course, just as normal as the bus trip to Forbes Field for a game. Going into a game, no one ever had a "We're-going-to-win" attitude. Instead, the feeling was, "I hope we don't lose." If they were in a close game and happened to get a bad break, nobody got charged-up, nobody tried harder.

Parker worked to change this attitude. "You guys expect to get beat," he screamed more than once. "You're giving games away. If the other team is going to win, at least make them earn it."

No sooner was the ink dry on Parker's contract, than he began a frenzied attempt to rebuild. It seemed that every time I went to practice there were new faces. There was a standing gag on the team not to send your laundry out because by the time it came back you were sure to be gone. All the backfield men were new. Parker brought in halfback Dick Young from the Colts, and Billy Wells, the other halfback, came from the Redskins. Fullback Bill Bowman had played for Parker at Detroit the previous season.

Big Ernie Stautner was our best defensive lineman. He never had a poor game. A tackle, he was a man of tremendous strength. The one-on-one block hardly bothered him and double teaming inconvenienced him only slightly. I remember him in the locker room and his bulging arm muscles and barrel chest with its massive bone structure. It made him appear as if he were equipped with plate armor.

Stautner was as relentless as any player I've ever known. I remember a game against the Cleveland Browns in which we were getting pounded, 45–10, and it was late in the fourth quarter. Most of us had one eye on the clock, hoping we'd soon be able to escape from public view. Not

Staunter. He just wouldn't quit. He played as tenaciously as if it were a close score in a crucial game. Shortly before it ended, he blasted through to trap the Cleveland quarterback in the end zone, then chased him and dropped him. That made the score 45–12. I always thought they should have given those two points to Stautner personally.

There were two rookie quarterbacks in camp when I arrived, Jack Kemp from Occidental College and Len Dawson from Purdue. But Parker quickly decided that I was his man and spent little time with the others and eventually he let both go. Kemp went on to lead the Buffalo Bills to a championship in the American Football League. Dawson did the same for the Kansas City Chiefs.

I had only six practice sessions behind me when we met the Washington Redskins in the opening game of the season. Parker really had everyone fired up and a Pittsburgh writer remarked we were so spirited that we looked like a visiting team.

The Redskins used a zone and had Gary Lowe, who had good size and strength but whose range of coverage was limited, playing cornerback. This proved a fatal weakness, for Gary had to cover Jug Girard, our fast and elusive split end. We'd run a couple of deep down-and-in patterns and then a quick down-and-out. Poor Gary; he didn't have much of a chance. We made several long gains and two touchdowns on him and won the game with ease.

Lowe had been a teammate of mine at Michigan State, so I felt bad when I learned that George Marshall, the Redskins' owner, was so enraged at his performance that he put Gary on waivers right after the game, and he didn't even bother to tell Joe Kuharich, the Washington coach, about it. The waivers expired, making Lowe a free agent.

Detroit then picked him up and he became a standout player with the Lions. So I guess I did him a favor.

Parker had a novel theory on how to win the league championship. He wanted his teams to be just off the pace until halfway through the season, then, in the stretch drive, make what he called "the big move." According to Buddy, most teams tried their hardest in September and October, only to fizzle out in the critical games of November and December.

The Steelers of 1957 followed Parker's strategy to the letter—for a time. Midway in the season, we were just off the pace, tied with the Giants for second place in the Eastern Conference standings with a 4–2 record. Cleveland was first. Parker was joyously optimistic. "We can beat anyone," he bragged.

Then came a game with Cleveland, one that everyone agreed would be the showdown contest of the season. Since they had lost only once and we had lost twice, it was a "must" game for us. Well, we moved the ball well, but made enough mistakes to last us the rest of the season. Twice we were in a position to score but an offside penalty killed one threat and a fumble ruined another. Some of the blunders were quite original. Once, one of our guys called for a fair catch and then let the ball bounce another twenty yards down the field. Another time, a punt of ours was about to roll dead when a Cleveland player stole the ball and got some good yardage. We lost, 24–0.

The slip-ups and our inability to get in the Cleveland end zone put Parker in a wretched mood. He kept the press out of the locker room after the game while he berated us. Most of what he said isn't printable.

The problem that existed was easy to perceive. Parker had a winning team in Detroit. He wanted a winner in

Pittsburgh, and he couldn't accept the fact that he didn't have the personnel to achieve one. Sure, we did well against Philadelphia, Washington, and Chicago (the Cardinals), but we weren't in the same class with Cleveland. We had no Jimmy Brown. The Steelers reacted to Parker's almost continual abuse by nosediving.

I had my own problems with him. During an early season game against the Cards, I suffered a pinched nerve in my neck. I had just handed off on a sweep when the defensive end came tearing in and gave me a shove. It was quite innocent, but his hands caught me low in the back, snapping my head like the lash of a whip. A stabbing pain flashed down my right hand and then the fingers went numb. The injury bothered me off and on for the rest of the season.

Everyone knows Vince Lombardi's philosophy about playing with small hurts. On the first day of practice of his first season as coach of the Packers, Lombardi walked into the trainer's room and there were fifteen or twenty players waiting to use the whirlpool bath and for diathermy treatment or rubdowns. Lombardi became enraged. "I have no patience with small hurts," he bellowed. "You've got to learn to live with small hurts and play with small hurts." The next day when Lombardi walked into the trainer's room there were only two or three men there.

I believe in Lombardi's "small hurts" philosophy. I think almost all players do. It is possible to psyche yourself, to transcend the pain of injury and play in spite of it.

But there are times a crippled player can hurt a team. After I was injured in that game against the Cards, almost every time a defenseman hit me the burning pain would rush down my arm and into my fingers. I couldn't raise

51

my arm high enough to hail a cab. And the pain was not the worst of it. The injury affected the nerves in my hand in such a way that I couldn't manipulate the fingers normally. As a result, there were a number of times that I had to take myself out of games for several plays, particularly on third down and long yardage situations when a pass was virtually the only possible call.

I'm sure Parker thought I was lacking in courage. He would glare at me when I came to the sidelines, and not say a word, just take a deep drag on his cigarette. Then he would turn his back and walk away from where I was standing.

After we dropped that crucial game to Cleveland, we lost to Green Bay, 27–10. This was two years before the dawn of the Lombardi era in Green Bay and the team that beat us was a bedraggled club, firmly settled in last place in the Western Conference. The game knocked us out of the Eastern Conference race and, just so there could be no doubt about it, we let ourselves get beaten by the Philadelphia Eagles the next week.

The next year brought more of the same. During the off-season, Parker sought to improve our running game through trades, and he brought in Tank Younger from the Los Angeles Rams and Tom Tracy, a stumpy halfback, from Detroit. But Younger, a nine-year veteran, showed his age, and Tracy was injured in an exhibition game.

Our preseason record was 2–4 and we opened the season on the West Coast against the Forty-Niners. We led, 20–7, in the third quarter, but San Francisco roared back and won, 23–20, on a last-ditch field goal. The plane trip back was really something.

The next week we played our first home game. We faced

the Browns and it was one of those days. We got belted, 45–12.

Buddy was livid after the game. He called a team meeting for the following day at the Roosevelt Hotel in Pittsburgh where the Steelers had their headquarters. Shortly before the meeting got underway, someone told me I was wanted on the telephone. It was Parker.

"We made a trade for you today," I heard him say. "You're going up to Detroit. We got Bobby Layne for you."

I was speechless. I really was. Finally I mumbled something about it being hard to believe.

When San Francisco traded me, I was stunned, too, but not like this. After all, the Forty-Niners had Tittle as their No. 1 man, and they had drafted Brodie, a local hero. I could understand why I wasn't needed. But in Pittsburgh it was different. I felt I was making a solid contribution. And there was something else. My wife and I had purchased a house in Pittsburgh, but before we signed the papers I had gone to Parker and asked about my future with the team, whether he had any plans to trade me or not. "Don't worry, kid," he had said. "You'll be here as long as I am."

After that telephone conversation, I never spoke to Parker again. The only time I ever saw him was when we played the Steelers, and sometimes I'd look across the field and catch a glimpse of him pacing the sidelines, and I knew he had a cigarette in his mouth and, if Pittsburgh was losing, I knew he'd be ranting.

CHAPTER SEVEN

After the trade was made, Parker held a press conference and told reporters that I wasn't his type of quarterback. "Morrall will never make it in this league," he said.

Bobby Layne personified Parker's type of quarterback. Of course, Layne's personality and mine were very different. I don't mean that in a pejorative sense; we're not the same, that's all. People often called Layne a "take charge guy." He was. He would take a team by the scruff of its neck, shake it a few times, and make it win.

But I question the tactics he used. Fear was his weapon. If he thought it was necessary, he ridiculed his teammates. He blasted and cursed them. A Pittsburgh reporter once called him a "hot-tempered mule skinner." Layne would scream at a guy during a game if he thought he had missed an assignment or wasn't putting out. "Get that sonavabitch off the field," he'd shriek. Parker always complied. I guess he was a little afraid of Layne, too.

Parker wanted me to be like this. I couldn't.

Just as important, I doubt the effectiveness of such tactics. While they may work with some players, others resent them. In fact, they feel degraded by them. They begin to press; they make mistakes. Some coaches use fear, too. Buddy Parker did. Vince Lombardi did.

When a team's winning, the players tend to overlook a coach's more abrasive traits. Success makes hardship bearable. But countless coaches have achieved success without berating or ranting at their players. They're perfectionists. They demand excellence in execution and they want the timing to be faultless. They're strict, however, and they make their players work. Paul Brown, now coach of the Cincinnati Bengals, is probably the best example of this type of leader. Don Shula is another coach in this mold.

When a team begins to lose, the players are quick to question the tactics and decisions of the authoritarian type coach. His rule becomes subverted. "What have I got to lose," a player figures. "If he trades me, the chances are fifty-fifty that I'll end up with a better team." But a player hates to leave a team that's winning.

Bobby Layne encountered these difficulties toward the end of his career. Many of the Pittsburgh players simply refused to put up with his abuse and asked to be traded.

There are other ways to lead besides the methods Layne used. I prefer to be confident rather than cocky, to display poise, not brass. Dignity is important, too.

It's difficult to enumerate all the factors that make an effective leader. Look at the quarterbacks in pro football—Unitas, Starr, Tarkenton, Namath, Meredith, Lamonica, and all the others. Each one has a different personality, and each goes about the business of leading in a slightly different way.

But the results they seek are always the same. A quarterback who truly leads is able to encourage teamwork and cooperation. He is able to persuade and motivate. He is able to bring about changes in behavior; that is, he is able to get the team to surpass itself, get the guys to play "over their heads."

Experience is one of the key factors in leadership. The number of successful rookie quarterbacks is as rare as field goals from the 50 yard line. Johnny Unitas was one of the very few quarterbacks who did well in his first year.

I think a player needs three to five years of seasoning in order to be effective in the National Football League.

It usually takes longer to be a winner, to quarterback a championship team. Again Unitas is the exception. When the Colts won the 1958 NFL title, Johnny was in his third year. It took Bart Starr six years with Green Bay, Frank Ryan seven years with Cleveland, and Billy Wade ten years with Chicago. Y. A. Tittle required twelve seasons before he quarterbacked a divisional winner.

A quarterback without pro experience makes mistakes. It never fails to happen. There's a greater chance he'll put the ball into a crowd, and he's less likely to throw the ball away, out of bounds or to an open spot, when the situation demands it. Things like that. Veteran players know when the rookie blunders. So not only is the error bad in itself, but it causes doubt, and, of course, doubt subverts one's ability to lead.

I know from my own experience that after you've been around for a while, the players are much more likely to accept you as a leader. When Bart Starr gets hit and fumbles, the players think, "Poor Bart; he *really* must have been hit." But when a rookie gets hit and fumbles, often the guys think, "What the hell's the matter with that guy? Doesn't he know how to hold onto the ball?"

Intelligence and understanding are important, too. You have to have a clear grasp of each play and this means you must know each player's responsibility on each play. I don't mean to say that you have to be able to draw accurately each player's assignment, but you have to have a mental picture of precisely what each play is meant to achieve, of how the backs are going to be set and whether the guards are going to be pulling or blocking. And then if someone misses an assignment, and you know it's his

56

fault, that he didn't slip or that he wasn't victimized by the opposition in some way, you can jump on him.

It's not just the quarterback; every topflight player has a complete understanding of what each play is meant to achieve. Sure, I know receivers who know the pattern they're supposed to run on each play, but that's all they know. They're usually very fast and they just run. But the better receivers know what their complementary receivers are supposed to do on each play, and they know where the backs are going. They also know exactly how the play is meant to take advantage of the defensive situation.

When I was in high school, my coach told me, "When you call the signals, don't be timid. Make damn sure everyone can hear." As a result I've always boomed the signals out in a powerful voice, like a Marine drill sergeant calling cadence. This, of course, is vital from a tactical standpoint; that is, you can't take a chance that a wide receiver is going to miss a signal. But a voice that's strong and commanding also helps to instill confidence in the team. If the signals are not distinct, or you hesitate, or there's the least bit of doubt in your voice, well, this can lead to your downfall.

The willingness to take suggestions is also important to successful quarterbacking. If an end comes into the huddle and tells me, say, that he can beat his man deep, the chances are good that I'll throw to him, not necessarily on the next play, but possibly on that series or the next series. Sometimes this can have spectacular results. Early in the 1968 season we were playing the Bears and we had the ball on about our 20, and Jimmy Orr came back to the huddle and announced, "I can beat my man on a down and out pattern. But wait," he said, "wait until we get to the 45 yard line. I want to score a touchdown." Well, we moved the ball to the Bears 48 and then I called the play. Jimmy threw a beautiful fake at their safety, like he was going down and in, then broke straight for the corner. I just laid it out there and Jimmy got his touchdown.

Of course, you can't take every suggestion from every receiver. You have to know your personnel. Some ends want the ball on every play. A man will come back and say to me, "I beat my man on the last play. Call that pattern again." Sure he beat his man, but he didn't realize he was double covered, that another man, the free safety perhaps, was also on him.

Linemen can also give you meaningful advice. A tackle will say, "My man's taking a wide rush," and he'll suggest running a draw play. Or he may say that his man is lining up real tight and he can turn him in. Or a guard may tell you that his man is barrelling in, charging straight ahead, and he'll ask for a trap.

Usually players give you ideas and advice while you're on the sidelines or when you're coming back to the huddle, but not in the huddle itself. The huddle is not an excuse for a group discussion. Once the huddle forms, I announce the formation and the play, and that's it. But sometimes I'll call a formation, setting up everyone but the receiver. Say it's a pattern to Jimmy Orr. Now Orr knows better than anyone else how his man is shading him. So I'll say to Jimmy, "What do you want?", and he'll answer, "I can beat him on a quick slant-in," or "I can beat him on a curl." As you can imagine, this intelligence has enormous value in putting together a successful pass.

It's no secret that confidence is to quarterbacking what skating is to ice hockey. Without it you're nothing. A quarterback's attitude is infectious. It quickly spreads to everyone on the squad. Any lack of confidence can be fatal. Once a team has doubts about the quarterback, it just won't go, even if he makes the soundest calls possible and executes like a virtuoso.

After I was traded by Parker, I spent seven seasons with the Detroit Lions. For one reason or another, I was on the bench a lot and they were often frustrating years. I saw clearly what can happen when a player, a quarterback, is robbed of his confidence, not only in my own case, but in several others. It's not a pretty thing.

CHAPTER EIGHT

After Buddy Parker abruptly quit the Lions not long before the opening of the 1957 season, Detroit elevated backfield coach George Wilson to the head coach's spot. Wilson, who had played end on the great Chicago Bears teams of the late 1930's and early 1940's, was a quiet and amiable person, known to everyone as a "nice guy." But once put in charge of the team, Wilson cracked down. He set a curfew and personally made bed checks to see that it was observed. A schedule of fines was posted for disciplinary infractions. And he worked the players as hard as they had ever been worked in their lives.

The Lions earned a 4—2 record during the exhibition season, but Wilson felt they had played uninspired football. So he got tougher. He had scarcely put his more stringent policies into effect when he got the news that Bobby Layne had been arrested on a drunken driving charge. Layne felt that he had been accused unjustly and decided to fight the charge in court. The Lion players attended the hearing *en masse*, and when a not guilty verdict was handed down, they cheered and stamped their feet. During the hearing, it was brought out that the arresting officer had been confused by Layne's Texas drawl, mistaking it for the garbled speech of an intoxicated person. After the hearing, the Lions held a not guilty party. The room they rented featured a huge banner made up by Friday Macklem, the team's equipment manager. It read: AH ALL AIN'T DRUNK; AH'M JUST FROM TEXAS.

Layne liked to party, a fact he never denied. Indeed,

he seemed bent upon living up to his reputation as a hell-raiser. Each year, just before training camp began, Layne and several of his cohorts would schedule one last fling. They'd hire a three-piece band and set out in a convertible with the top down and the band blaring and make the rounds of their favorite watering holes. They virtually took over every place they visited. Layne did the same in Pittsburgh.

Wilson weathered such antics wonderfully well. He got the team into contention early and kept them winning with a high degree of consistency despite injuries to key players. The most serious blow came in the next to last game of the season. The Lions faced the Browns. In the second quarter, Layne was buried in a pileup and came out of the tangle of bodies with his leg broken in three places. This figured to be the end of the road for the Lions, but veteran quarterback Tobin Rote, who had been obtained earlier in the season as insurance, filled in beautifully. He guided the Lions to a win in the final game of the season and to a playoff victory over the Forty-Niners. Then came the championship game and again Rote starred as the Lions buried the Cleveland Browns in a landslide, 59–14.

I've given this background to indicate the climate that prevailed when I arrived upon the scene. Bobby Layne, who had gone to Pittsburgh, was still something of a hero because he had quarterbacked the Lions into contention the year before. Tobin Rote, who had taken over when Layne was injured and brought the Lions the championship, was a hero, too. He was also the No. 1 quarterback.

Wilson, once a hero, was not held in high esteem because he had traded Layne away. In the teams' first appearance at Briggs Stadium that year, one group of fans displayed a banner that declared in no uncertain terms, TRADE WILSON.

As for me, I was not exactly a glory figure. People had a "wait and see attitude" toward me, I think.

There were certain advantages in playing for Wilson. For one, he always looked at things from the viewpoint of the players. Like he saw to it that the team always traveled first class and stayed in the better hotels. When a player would get involved in a controversy with the front office, Wilson would sometimes support the player. He'd often allow players to bring guests to training camp for lunch or dinner. In general, he sought to treat us as he would have liked to be treated had he been a member of the team.

Undoubtedly this attitude stemmed from his long experience as a player with the Chicago Bears. He was with the team in their glory days when they were known as the "Monsters of the Midway." George, an end, took part in the Bears' classic 73–0 shellacking of the Washington Redskins in the 1940 championship playoff; in fact, he played an important role in the game.

The Bears received the opening kickoff and after running one play to probe the Redskin defenses, they lined up for second down on their own 32 yard line. They operated out of a straight T. George McAfee, the Bears' right halfback, went in motion to the right. Quarterback Sid Luckman took the snap from center, faked a handoff to Ray Nolting, and then pitched to Bill Osmanski who picked up a key block from George Musso and swept wide around right end. Chicago blockers flattened one Washington defenseman after another and Osmanski kept rolling.

He was at about the 30 yard line when two Washington players, Ed Justice and Jimmy Johnston, thundered in from the side. Wilson had run completely across the field, and was there. He hurled his body into the air to block out Justice, and Justice collided with Johnston. Both fell as if they had been bludgeoned by a blunt instrument. Later, George Halas called it "the greatest, the most vicious block I ever saw." Osmanski scored. The game was only fifty-five seconds old and the Bears were on their way to one of the most one-sided victories football, pro or otherwise, has ever known.

After the game. Osmanski shared a cab with George and his wife.

"Congratulations, Bill, on your wonderful run," said Mrs. Wilson.

Osmanski grinned.

"And that was quite a block that cleared the way for you," she continued. "By the way, who threw it?"

Wilson's answer has not been recorded, but I'm sure I know some of the words he used.

Wilson was in his late forties when I joined the team. He was big—six-foot-one, 240—but still athletic looking. He looked like he still might be able, on a good day, to outrun a defensive back.

Detroit's defense at the time, often rated as pro football's best, was bulwarked by Joe Schmidt, our middle linebacker. This was a period in which the opposition often sought to bewilder the middle linebacker by sending two receivers out to encircle him. And on a rush, he would often be double-teamed. But such tactics rarely worked against Joe. He could diagnose what was coming better than anyone else I ever knew. He could also pursue, move laterally, and tackle like a demon. He was particularly effective on hook passes, where a receiver breaks downfield, then suddenly darts back a few steps. He was devastating on the blitz, and would roar through the line like a truck on the Edsel Ford Expressway. Joe, an All Pro selection eight times, became the Lions head coach in 1967.

Schmidt was flanked by two standouts in Wayne Walker and Carl Brettschneider. Ends Darris McCord and Sam Williams gave us both strength and mobility outside. Alex Karras, and his 300-pound running mate, Roger Brown, were incomparable tackles.

Karras had startling quickness and mobility. He was big—six-foot-two, 245 pounds. But his weight was concentrated in his upper body. He had a massive chest and arms. His legs, in comparison, looked almost spindly, and this is what gave him his agility. We called him "Twinkle-toes" because he moved around with such high stepping grace. I've played basketball with him—he played guard—and he could move up and down the court with the ease of a track man.

Karras was the team's funnyman. In training camp or when the team was on the road, he often provided uproarious mealtime entertainment with imaginative, impromptu routines. Once he did a parody on tedious award banquets that professional athletes attend so frequently. He'd get everyone's attention by clinking a knife handle on a water glass. When it was quiet, he'd begin: "Podunk High is proud to present these trophies to its players, the players' mothers, the cheerleaders, to the janitors who sweep the gym floor, and the firemen who forbid us to smoke in the grandstand.

"We know you've been here for three and a half hours," he'd say, "but we know you wouldn't want to leave without hearing a few words from our Superintendent of Schools." Then he'd take up the role of the Superintendent and give a short whimsical speech. And he used such occasions to needle the players and the coaches. Joe Schmidt got it for his German heritage—Karras called him *Herr Schmidt*—Carl Brettschneider was on the receiving end for his receding hairline, and Darrell Sanders, a tackle, for the white streak in his hair; Karras nicknamed him Skunk.

During the 1968 season, the Lions once went eleven consecutive quarters without scoring a touchdown and Karras made the failing the subject of a locker room lecture. Standing on a stool, he held a football high above his head, and shouted out, "Look here! Look here!" Then he spoke slowly, emphasizing every syllable. "This is what we know as a football. What you must do is throw it, run with it, walk with it, crawl with it—you can do anything—but you must get the football across the three-inch white line at the end of the field and into an area that is ten yards deep and one hundred and sixty feet wide and called the end zone. Then you will have scored what is known as a touchdown. An official will raise his hands over his head signaling the fact that your team is to be credited with six points. The fans," Alex concluded, "will then applaud."

I had always thought I was a pretty fair punter until I went to the Lions. I had punted in high school and in college, and I continued to punt when I joined the Forty-Niners. I averaged thirty-nine yards per punt for the season. At Pittsburgh, Jug Girard did the punting and I was his backup man. Then I went to Detroit and I met the Lions punter, Yale Lary. The first time I saw him kick I just stood open-mouthed. He was uncanny. He boomed the ball so high and so far that he gave me the feeling that he knew something about the art that no one else knew, some secret piece of information. Whenever we practiced kicking together, I came away with the feeling that

I shouldn't have left the dressing room. Lary led the league in punting an unprecedented three times, in 1959, 1961, and 1963.

But instead of causing my retirement as a kicker, Lary's proficiency opened up a new vista for me. I became Detroit's "short kicker." It worked like this: suppose a punting situation came up with the ball on the opponent's 45 yard line. If Larry punted, he was quite likely to put the ball into the end zone, and the opposition would have it first and ten on their 20. So they'd send me in to kick. I'd give it all I had but the ball never reached the end zone. It would go high, drop almost straight down, and hardly roll at all. Quite a few times it stopped dead inside the opposition's 5 yard line.

I had been with the team about a week when Wilson used me in a game against the Rams. I worked a bootleg that got us seven yards, and then I completed a pass to Hop Cassady that was good for a touchdown. This tied the score, 21–21.

Late in the fourth period, Wilson put me in a second time and I passed eighteen yards to Gene Gedman to tie the score again at 28–28. I heard cheers—but not for long. With about two minutes left, we had the ball on third down on the Rams' 22. A field goal would have put us ahead. In came a play from the bench—a pass. Jack Morris intercepted for Los Angeles and carried the ball to midfield. Two plays later the Rams scored. When we fumbled the ensuing kickoff, they scored again. That made it 42–28 and that's the way it ended.

Later in the season Wilson gave me the starting assignment against the Rams on the West Coast. We won, but it was a woeful day for me because I suffered a slight shoulder separation. It was a week before I could throw the ball again and the pain was pretty bad. I got so that I could throw long pretty well, but short passes, which you have to snap off, caused the shoulder to hurt even more.

Wilson used me only in spot assignments for the rest of the season. The whole year was pretty much a washout.

CHAPTER NINE

After I had joined the Colts late in 1968 and we had won a few games, and the fans had gotten to know me some, quite a few of them said to me, "We didn't know if we could ever get to like you, Earl, not after what you did to us in 1960."

They were referring to an incredible game that had a fantastic finish. It sticks out in the memory of anyone who happened to see it.

The game was played in Baltimore and Memorial Stadium, always a pressure cooker to play in, was jammed to the rafters. Remember, the Colts had won the league championship in 1958 and 1959, and the fans were hungry for them to do it again. We had beaten the Colts earlier in the year, so there was also a revenge angle involved.

The early scoring was a bit bizarre, with the points coming in small clusters, like runs in a baseball game. The Colts took a 2–0 lead in the opening minutes on a blocked punt that caromed into our end zone. We moved ahead on a field goal later in the period. Then the Colts came back on a sideline pass from Unitas to Lenny Moore that resulted in a touchdown. That made it 8–3, Colts.

Jim Ninowski was our starting quarterback, but in the fourth quarter, with the score still 8–3, Wilson sent me in. There were about eight minutes left to play. The first pass I tried was good for a touchdown, but the play had a freakish twist. I floated the ball deep to Hop Cassady and he caught it at about the Colts two yard line, then turned to run. Immediately he slammed into the goal posts.

He hit so hard he bounced back and then he circled and staggered drunkenly into the end zone a second time. As he came off the field, I clapped him on the back and said, "Way to go, Hoppy! Nice catch!" But he went right by me without even nodding. Then I realized the poor guy was out on his feet. He didn't know where he was or what was happening. His head cleared while he was sitting on the bench and they told him he had scored a touchdown.

A few minutes later, Jim Martin kicked a field goal from our 47 yard line. Now it was 13–8 in our favor. There were about two minutes left.

Two minutes, however, were enough for Unitas. He brought the Colts down the field in seven or eight plays and then threw to Lenny Moore who made an unbelievable catch. Night Train Lane was covering Moore and kept with him stride for stride. Then Night Train turned back to look for the ball and as he did, it sailed right by him. Moore dove with his arms outstretched, getting just his fingertips on the ball, but with Moore that was enough. He landed on his belly in the end zone, the ball firmly in his grasp.

Well, you should have seen the Baltimore fans. They came pouring out of the stands and down onto the field, and they pounded Lenny Moore on the back, and then picked him up and handed him back into the stands, like they do a bag of peanuts or a hot dog from a vendor. And they were jumping up and down and making more noise than I had ever heard before in my life. Finally, the officials got the fans across the sidelines and Steve Myhra booted the extra point. Now Baltimore was ahead, 15–13.

Again the crowd mobbed out onto the field and they tore down the goal posts. There must have been about ten thousand of them. "Please, please," came the voice of the public address announcer. "There are only ten seconds left. This is one of Baltimore's finest hours; let's not spoil it by having to forfeit the game. Please clear the field." The fans went to the sidelines.

Bruce Maher brought the kickoff out to our 35 yard line. The play was about over when a Baltimore player—I think it was Lebron Shields—piled into Steve Junker while Steve was on one knee, and the impact rolled Steve over a couple of times. I grabbed an official, pointed to Shields, and screamed, "He can't do that! He can't do that!" The official threw his flag down, but before he actually called the penalty Carl Brettschneider, one of our linebackers, dashed out on the field and kicked Shields. Another official saw that. So the first penalty was offset by the second and the ball stayed on the 35.

To win, all we needed was a field goal, and if we could get across midfield we'd be in range because Jim Martin, our kicker, was capable of making the long ones. A fifteen-yard play was what we needed. I planned to try a pass, then call a time-out to stop the clock. We had all our time-outs left.

When we came out onto the field, an official was standing over the ball. "Are you going to start the clock when you walk away from there?" I asked. "Yeh," he said. "O.K.," I answered, "Time out."

The crowd was really raising the roof, and when we huddled I had to shout the play to be heard. I called "three left, green right, eight right"—a play that would riddle their secondary with decoys, with Jim Gibbons, our strong side end, the receiver over the middle.

The ball was snapped and when I dropped back to setup, I could see the whole thing forming, just as if Wilson were diagramming it on the blackboard. Gail Cogdill, our split

70

end, cut from the right side and took three men with him, opening up the middle. Ken Webb, our fullback, ran a slant and took a linebacker. Hop Cassady went deep and two men went with him. Gibby raced straight down about fifteen yards, then cut to the middle. He had to go up to get the ball but he got it—a fine catch. He ducked to get away from their safety and the man went over Gibby's back, colliding with the other safety who had been about to make the tackle.

Then Gibby streaked for the sidelines to get out of bounds and stop the clock, but when he got over there no one was around, so he turned and raced for the end zone. Bob Boyd was the only man who chased him, but Ken Webb, who had seen the catch, came up to protect Gibby and he shouldered Boyd away. Carl Taseff, one of the defensemen who had gone deep with Cogdill, also might have had a chance to bring Gibby down, but Cogdill blocked him out.

When Gibby crossed the 20 yard line, the gun went off ending the game, but none of us heard it because of the noise. Then Gibby crossed into the end zone and the crowd suddenly went silent, just like they had all been struck dumb all at once.

We lined up to kick the extra point. I looked up at the stands and they were just about empty. More thousands were now on the field and they completely surrounded us. They stood there, not moving, not saying a word, like people at a cemetery. I didn't know what was going to happen. It was scary. I knelt on one knee to get the snap from center. Before I began the count, an official in back of me leaned over and said, "When you kick that point, run for the locker room. And don't stop." He didn't need to tell me.

71

Martin kicked the point and we jogged off the field. No one touched us. Hardly a word was said. The people were numb. Too much had happened in too short a time. With fifteen seconds to play, we were leading, 13–8. With fourteen seconds to play, they led, 15–13. And in the end we won, 20–15. No wonder the fans were in shock.

The defeat so stunned the Colt team they never recovered. Instead of taking over first place in the standings, they fell into a tie with Green Bay and San Francisco. They had two more games on their schedule and they lost them both.

I will never forget that game. I will never forget Gibby throwing the ball into the air after he scored, nor the sudden, eerie stillness of the crowd, nor the wide grins and back slaps in the dressing room, and then the triumphant flight home, when we savored every detail. Games like that make up for the physical grind, the injuries and the frustrations. Games like that are what keep you coming back.

CHAPTER TEN

One time my wife drove to a Detroit home game with Betsy Rote, Tobin's wife. "I'm so thrilled," my wife said, "because Earl's starting today."

Betsy gave her a puzzled look. "Earl's starting? Why George told Tobin that he was starting."

That's the way it was in Detroit. No one ever knew.

Before the season opened each year, Wilson would declare, "The quarterback job is open. It all depends on who looks the best."

But even if you opened the regular season at quarterback, it didn't mean too much. He might yank you out of there at any time. It depended on what happened in practice during the week.

And even if you won a starting assignment, that didn't mean much either. Wilson was forever shifting players— the ends, the offensive backs and especially the quarterbacks. Everything was all right if you had the game going well, but the minute something went wrong—bang—you were out of there. That's the way it was for seven years in Detroit—in and out, in and out all the time.

The system was a horror. It robbed me—and the other quarterbacks, too—of the willingness to take a chance. I always found myself going with the percentage play, no matter what the situation. I felt in that way I was much less likely to get second-guessed. But a quarterback has to be able to innovate. He has to be able to gamble. The defense plays percentages, and if you can't cross them up once in a while with a tricky call, then you're handing them a tremendous advantage. A quarterback just has to be able to throw the dice now and then.

Suppose you had a third and two situation. The percentage call is to send one of your backs into the line. But once in a while you just might want to throw long to cross up the defense. Well, with George Wilson coaching, if you threw long when it was third and two and it didn't work, you'd find yourself sitting on the bench for the rest of the game. And maybe the next game, too. So you didn't throw long very often when it was third and two.

You had no freedom; you had no way to throw the defense off balance. They saw our films. They knew what was going on. They knew when it was third and two that we'd be running. They were absolutely certain of it, and they were able to adjust accordingly.

During the 1959 season, Wilson shuttled me in and out of the line-up with Tobin Rote. The club finished 3–8–1. It was Rote's last year with the Lions. He had been having contract problems with the club, so he played out his option in 1959, then joined a team in the Canadian league. Naturally I looked upon this as a break, figuring I was pretty well set for the coming year. Not a chance. During the off season, the club traded to get Jim Ninowski from the Browns. I knew Jim well. He was a sophomore at Michigan State when I was in my senior year. After he graduated, he was drafted by the Browns and he became Cleveland's No. 2 quarterback behind Milt Plum. Ninowski liked to pass the ball, and he loved to pass long. If he had been a baseball player, he'd have swung for the fences on every trip to the plate.

With the club's acquisition of Ninowski, I realized the quarterback job was wide open again, and that we'd go to camp and whoever did the best in pre-season games would get the starting job. I seldom do well in pre-season play—I can't explain why—and 1960 was no exception. Ninowski became the starter. I got in mostly to hold the ball on extra point attempts. I threw the ball only about twenty times up until that fantastic game with Baltimore.

After we beat the Colts, Wilson told me that I was to be the starting quarterback. We were 5–5 at the time, and Green Bay and Chicago were ahead of us, both with 6–4 records. The next week we whipped the Dallas Cowboys in the bitter cold at Briggs Stadium and I completed twelve of fourteen passes, one for a touchdown. The team was moving at full gallop now, and the following week we tore apart the Bears, 36–0, and this was a team that had beaten us earlier in the season.

Unfortunately, Green Bay kept on winning, too, and so our late-season heroics got us no higher than second place. They didn't do me much good either. The next season Wilson went back to platooning me with Ninowski.

A quarterback is so vital to a team's success that every club must carry at No. 2 man in case the starting man is injured. This is as basic to pro football as a ball and goalposts. The Packers serve as a good example of the contribution a skilled substitute can make, for they took three consecutive NFL titles beginning in 1965 partly because Zeke Bratkowski filled in so efficiently anytime Bart Starr was injured. My point is that the role of the No. 2 man must be clearly defined as that of an understudy. He and the No. 1 man should not be competitive, not once the regular season begins. Coaches do realize this, of course. Almost always the backup man is a veteran, a player whose best days are already in the record books. Babe Parilli of the New York Jets is a case in point; George Blanda of the Raiders is another.

If the backup quarterbacks of pro football ever form a Hall of Fame of their own, I'm sure the first man elected would be George Ratterman. He was No. 2 at Notre Dame behind Johnny Lujack, and he held the same status with the Cleveland Browns for most of his years as a pro, since he had the misfortune of having his career parallel that of Otto Graham's. Yet being a perennial backup man seldom seemed to bother Ratterman; in fact, he got a kick out of it. He once said that being successful in football without really playing was something of an art form, almost as difficult as actually playing, although not nearly as physically damaging. One season he took to walking with a fake limp, just so he'd look like one of the boys.

However, Ratterman was sometimes distressed by Coach Paul Brown's attitude toward him. "The thought of using me seemed to strike the Cleveland coach as comical," George once said.

Ratterman's most demeaning moment came one November afternoon when the Browns were playing the Forty-Niners. Graham was having a rare off-day. Late in the third quarter, San Francisco intercepted one of his passes and a sprinkling of fans began to howl. "We want Ratterman! We want Ratterman!" The cries were just barely audible, Ratterman recalls.

Brown heard the fans, too, and he beckoned Ratterman. George quickly peeled off his canvas hood, grabbed his unmarked helmet, and approached the coach for instructions. He felt sure that in a moment he'd be in the midst of the fray.

Brown put his hand on Ratterman's shoulder and looked him squarely in the eye. "George," he said, "your friends are calling for you." Then, pausing for dramatic effect he added, "Maybe you'd better go up there and sit in the stands for a while."

Often the rivalry for a quarterback post can develop into antagonism. Bobby Layne's best days in Detroit came when he was backed up by fellows like Jim Hardy, Tom Dublinski, and Harry Gilmer. When Tobin Rote, more highly esteemed than any of these, arrived upon the scene, a troublesome period began, and it ended only when Layne was dispatched to Pittsburgh.

Los Angeles tried using two quarterbacks of about equal skill in Bob Waterfield and Norm Van Brocklin. The result was open hostility. When Waterfield retired, the club paired Van Brocklin with Bill Wade and the system failed again.

The Green Bay Packers once had a two-quarterback situation. They had Lamar McHan, who Vince Lombardi had obtained from the Chicago Cardinals, and Bart Starr. After the 1960 NFL championship game, in which Norm Van Brocklin guided the Philadelphia Eagles to a 17–13 win over the Packers, there were rumors that Lombardi was unhappy with Starr, that he was in the market for a tried and proven quarterback, which Starr at the time was not. Then, not long before the 1961 season opened, Lombardi traded McHan to the Redskins. He was saying, in effect, "Bart Starr is No. 1 at Green Bay." Starr says this really boosted his confidence, that it helped him tremendously in achieving the eminence he now enjoys.

After the 1961 season, Ninowski was returned to Cleveland in exchange for Milt Plum, who had been the league's leading passer in 1960 and 1961. Milt was six-foot-two, 210, just about my height and build, but slope-shouldered. He was prim and mild-mannered, the type of person you'd expect to find teaching English literature to the youngsters

77

at Cranbrook, the very proper prep school near Detroit that the Lions used as a training base. We were both about the same age and both had the same amount of experience. Plum was more the technician, however; more concerned with methods and tactics. It really wasn't in character for him to play the role of a leader—not to a group of grizzled football veterans, at any rate—and when he had to chastize a lineman for, say, missing a block, his high-pitched voice won him only grins. He had good friends on the team, but as a rule he remained aloof from the players.

Plum was superb in training camp his first season with the club. Thus, I was assigned to the bench. I spent most of my time on the phones, usually in contact with Scooter McLean, one of the assistant coaches, who was posted in the press box. He'd relay information to me on the defensive setups the opposition was using, and I'd talk to our defensive players when they came off the field, and try to determine what the opposition linemen were doing. Were they stunting or slanting their charges? Were their linebackers blitzing? And I'd talk to the receivers to try to find out just how they were being covered and to learn what patterns they thought might work.

Naturally, if I got into the game I'd put this information to use. If I didn't play, I'd talk to Ninowski or, later, Plum, on the sidelines and try to help him. But you have to be careful. In one game I remember a receiver telling me that he could beat his man on a quick slant-in pattern. So I told Plum and he said he'd use it. The next time we got possession and the teams lined up, I could see the middle linebacker had moved over a couple of steps to one side and the quick slant-in was no longer quite so good a call. But Plum didn't notice the adjustment and when he ran the play the linebacker easily batted down the ball; in fact, he almost made an interception. When Plum came off the field he gave me a funny look. What I'm saying is that sometimes it's best to let the quarterback play his own game, call his own plays, and merely make yourself available to provide information he might ask for. The quarterback is on the receiving end of an endless stream of facts from the head coach, the assistant coach and the players on the field with him. Too much information just confuses things.

Whatever chance Plum had to achieve top-flight status with the Lions was destroyed one afternoon early in the 1962 season. We were playing the Packers. It was a key game, for the Packers figured to be our chief competition for the Western Conference title that year.

We were leading, 7–6, in the closing minutes of the game, and we had the ball on our own 22. Plum was moving the team up the field smartly, mixing ground and pass plays cleverly. Twice on third down and long yardage situations he had connected. But should he have been risking any passes at all? Probably not. Green Bay needed only a field goal to win. Since the ball was deep in our own territory, an interception could have brought disaster.

At any rate, Plum worked the ball to our 49. It was third down. There was one minute and forty-six seconds left to play. The percentage call was a running play. Even if it didn't gain enough for a first down, we had Yale Lary to punt. It's likely that Lary would have booted the ball into their end zone, giving the Packers first and ten on their 20 with about a minute to play. Then they would have had to face a well-rested defense that most observers judged to be the best in the league.

Well, Plum elected to pass, to try for another first down, and he called a down-and-out pattern to Terry Barr. Herb

79

Adderly, the Packers' left cornerback, was sitting back and waiting. The ball was off target and Adderly made an easy interception and then, picking up blocking, raced all the way to our 22. A couple of plays later Hornung booted the game-winning field goal.

It was a very costly loss. If we had won that game we would have ended the season in a tie with Green Bay for the conference title. As it was, we had to be content with the Playoff Bowl. The defeat caused great bitterness, and I think it was a turning point in Plum's stay with Detroit. Some of the members of the defensive unit never got over it. Through the balance of the season, whenever the defensive team came off the field and they passed the offensive team going on, Joe Schmidt would say to Plum, "Pass, Milt, three times, and then punt."

Of course, the weekly competition that Wilson staged to find the quarterback with the hottest arm did not help Plum any. When he did get the starting assignment, and he got more of them than I did, he said he'd often find himself looking over his shoulder to see if I was warming up. If he didn't do it literally, he did it figuratively. He was always uneasy about my presence.

The quarterback situation at Detroit was bad enough in itself, but it was worsened by the treatment the team and some of the players received at the hands of the press. I do believe that it is within the province of a newspaper reporter to criticize. My point is that in Detroit it was always overdone. The whole attitude of the press contrasted sharply with what I found later in New York and then in Baltimore. In each of those cities, the newspapers had a positive attitude toward their teams. Sure, they found fault and they criticized, but they never seemed intent upon tearing down the team's whole structure.

Indeed, there were problems in Detroit. There were disputes in the front office. There was an ugly gambling incident (in which Alex Karras was suspended for a year and four other members of the team were fined). And there was the game of musical chairs for the quarterback spot. But I'm sure the press made each of these situations seem worse than they actually were.

Quarterbacks, of course, are special victims of the second guess, and the Detroit newspapers made this one of their specialties. If a truck driver makes a mistake, the insurance company takes the rap and the guy is back at work the next day. If a surgeon makes a wrong cut, the blunder winds up in the hospital morgue, and no one ever accuses him of any lack of competence. But just let a quarterback make what seems to be a bad call, and all hell breaks loose.

I really don't mean this to sound like a complaint. It's an observation, no more. I consider being second-guessed as part of the job, like having my ankles taped before a game. But most criticism isn't justified. A quarterback calling a game knows a great deal more about what's happening than the people on the sidelines, the fans or the guys in the pressbox. He might know, for instance, that the back who usually carries for two or three yards is so beat that he can hardly hold his head up. He may know that the time is right to hit an end. He may be under orders to go with a play that's been sent in from the bench.

"Mr. Inconsistent" was one of the names the press tagged me with in Detroit. They said I was likely to be good one day and awful the next. I remember one headline in 1962 that read: RECORD OF INCONSISTENCY STILL HAUNTS MORRALL.

It's really an injustice to brand any quarterback as inconsistent. Of course, he can be more effective one week

81

than he is the next, but this applies to people in every profession. Even your insurance man has good days and not so good.

In the case of a quarterback, there are usually reasons for any drastic change in performance. How could a quarterback of Joe Namath's skills, in the same year that he led the Jets to the pro football championship, throw five interceptions against teams like Denver and Buffalo? This doesn't mean that Namath, by nature, is inconsistent. It can happen that the guys who are supposed to defend you have off days. When your pocket protection breaks down, you're under constant pressure. You have no time. Then there are days that receivers drop passes. But it's only the quarterback who is singled out for criticism, at least that's the way it seems. He's the only one who is said to be guilty of lack of consistency.

One newspaper in Detroit called me the "quarterback who cannot start." But coming off the bench, I was said to be superb. They tagged me the best "game-saving quarterback in pro football." I thought that this was just plain foolish.

The papers never stopped, but I tried not to let their criticism bother me. I never felt I was inconsistent. I never felt that I was second best or second rate. I was certain that any time Wilson would hand me the football and say, "O.K Earl, you're my No. 1 quarterback," I'd do a standout job.

In 1963, he did.

Plum started the first five games of the season and then came up with a bad elbow. (PLUM OUT; LIONS STUCK WITH MORRALL, one newspaper declared.) Wilson made me the No. 1 man, a status I was to hold for the balance of the season. In my first start, we played the Colts and were leading, 21–18, in the closing minutes when Wilson took me out and sent Plum in and he passed just once. Andy Nelson intercepted and he went for a touchdown. Now Plum had more than a sore elbow to worry about. I started again the next week and threw three touchdown passes against Minnesota, and four the next week against San Francisco.

I had now been with the Lions six years, but never had the offense clicked so well. We had some real scoring splurges. Yet injuries ruined any hope we might have had for a championship. Linebacker Joe Schmidt was out of action for a month with a shoulder separation, and Schmidt was as vital to our defense as lights are to a night game. On top of this, Karras was sitting out his suspension.

Five key men—flanker Pat Studstill, linebacker Carl Brettschneider, defensive halfback Gary Lowe, offensive halfback Larry Ferguson, and defensive end Darris McCord—underwent surgery. At one time, three of our four defensive backs were on the sidelines. The club, out of desperation, coaxed Hop Cassady out of retirement to serve as a defensive replacement, and on the first play of the first game he played, he pulled a hamstring muscle. It was that kind of a year. We had about twenty-five players who missed at least one game because of injuries, which must be some kind of a record. Someone said we had every type of ailment but snakebite.

Nevertheless, we were a tough club to beat. Green Bay and Chicago were battling for the Western Conference championship, and Cleveland was a leading contender in the East, and we played all three of them toward the end of the season.

Green Bay was beating us, 13–6, when we took over the ball on our own 22 with about nine minutes remaining in the game. I mixed the plays as well as I had ever done in my life, hitting Terry Barr and Gail Cogdill on passes, mostly short stuff, and handing to Nick Pietrosante and Dan Lewis who spearheaded the ground game. We were as unstoppable as falling water. With twenty-eight seconds to play, we had the ball, third down on the Packer half-yard line. Pietrosante took it in and we got a tie.

The next week we knocked the Browns out of the Eastern Conference race, and the following week we came close to doing the same to the Bears in the West.

It was my finest year in professional football up to that time. I passed for 2,621 yards, a new club record. The previous mark had been held by Bobby Layne. I completed 174 passes in 328 attempts for a 53.0 percentage, and twenty-four of the passes went for touchdowns. The players, in a secret vote, named me the team's most valuable player.

I proved a lot of things to myself that year, but I guess I didn't prove anything to Wilson. When we went to training camp the following summer, he said that Plum and I would have to fight it out again. I played to my usual pre-season form. When the season opened, I was back on the bench.

Once that season Wilson decided who was to be the starting quarterback by the flip of a coin. He really did. It was about half an hour before game time, and he got Milt and me together and he tossed a coin in the air.

"Call it," he said to Milt.

Milt called heads. That's how it came up.

CHAPTER ELEVEN

I have one nightmarish memory of 1964. We were playing the Bears, a team that did a lot of red dogging. It was the sixth game of the season.

Chicago had this six-foot-eight, 280-pound defensive end named Doug Atkins, a real super-human. Or maybe "inhuman" is a better word. His nickname was "Frankenstein." From the back he always looked to me like a well-stuffed silo.

On a third down and long yardage play, I went back to pass and they really blasted in. Joe Fortunato, an outside linebacker, timing the count perfectly, broke with the snap, and looped around to drive up the middle. Our center, Bob Whitlow, was occupied with their middle linebacker, and I could see Fortunato, a big guy, breeze right through. Out of instinct I ducked to one side so that our fullback, Nick Pietrosante, could pick him up. Nick hit Fortunato hard but didn't dump him. Now I had to unload—quickly.

I looked for Jim Gibbons who was supposed to be out in the flat, but Gibby had been tripped up and was sprawled on the ground. Fortunato was loose. As I rolled out I spotted Danny Lewis slanting into the flat. I stopped and cocked my arm, but Danny Lewis wouldn't look my way. "Look, Danny! Look, Danny!" He never turned. Fortunato hit me low, getting one arm around my knees.

Then, while my legs were pinned, Atkins struck. I never saw him coming but he felt like a Sherman tank. He hit me chest high, toppling me over backwards. I landed on my right shoulder, and then Atkins came crashing down on top of me, an experience that must be something like having a brick building fall on you. When I hit the ground, the pain was bad, as if someone had stabbed me in front at about the base of the neck.

After we untangled ourselves, I got to my feet and I tried to move my right arm and this terrific pain knifed through my shoulder. When I ran off the field, I just let the arm hang down limply at my side. The team doctor came rushing up to me and made me sit down on the bench. He tried to get his hand up under my shoulder pads to find out what was wrong but he couldn't. "Let's go into the locker room so we can get a look at this," he said.

"Hell, no. I'm O.K.," I protested. I wasn't being heroic. I really didn't think there was anything seriously wrong.

"Look at this," I said, and I held the arm out straight, and then to the side, and then reached across my body with it. "There's nothing wrong with it."

The doctor persisted. He raised my jersey up around my neck, then wedged his hand underneath the shoulder pad on the right side. Suddenly he drew it away. I looked at his face for some indication of what he'd found. "Let's go into the locker room," he said.

"You're crazy," I said. "I'm O.K."

And then, without saying anything, he took my left hand and slipped it beneath the shoulder pads. "Go easy," he said. Then I felt it, a sharp point like the tip of an arrow underneath the skin—the broken end of my collarbone.

I decided I would go into the locker room.

The healing process was long and painful. Through the fall and deep into the winter, the shoulder was still giving me a great deal of trouble. That spring I considered quitting football, the first time I ever seriously entertained such thoughts.

The doctors assured me, however, that the bone had knit perfectly, but when I played handball and tried to slam a shot overhand, I could hardly pull the arm through, the pain was so intense. I went to Lansing in the spring to work out with the Michigan State football team, and when I tried to pass the ball I found that I couldn't throw more than ten yards or so. The muscles in my shoulder became so tender that just moving the arm became a trial. And I couldn't get any zip on the ball. My passes looked like they were thrown by a schoolgirl.

During the early summer I worked out at the University of Detroit two or three times a week and slowly the arm began to come around. By the time the training season rolled around, I was able to get the ball out fifty yards or so and the pain was almost gone. I knew it was going to be O.K.

CHAPTER TWELVE

During the seven years I spent with the Lions, there were a number of times that the brawling among stockholders and team officials outdid the scuffling on the field at Tiger Stadium. Eventually the front office wrangling led to the departure of George Wilson and soon after George left, so did I.

Wilson's job was first in jeopardy in 1959, a season in which the club finished with a 3–8–1 record. The Lions had won the league championship just two years before, remember. The club was then owned by 144 shareholders, and at times it seemed that about 143 of them were yelling for poor George's scalp. But Edwin J. (Andy) Anderson, then the club president, went to bat for George and saved his job.

Not long after, George got a chance to return the favor. In 1961, D. Lyle Fife, a former president of the club, sought to oust Anderson from his post, and he went about lining up stockholder support. The attempt failed and one important reason it did was because Wilson wrote a 600-word letter to each of the 144 stockholders—it became known as "Wilson's White Paper"—in which he came out flatly for Anderson.

Andy stayed on. William Clay Ford, a vice president and director of the Ford Motor Company, and a grandson of Henry Ford, became the club's new president. (All the players started driving guess what kind of car.) In 1964, Ford acquired the stock in the club, ending the rule of the 144.

George wanted to move into a management post with the Lions. I'm sure that was his ambition. But Ford brought in Russ Thomas, a one-time tackle for the Lions, and later a scout, to be general manager. This embittered Wilson and open warfare was the result. If we had a road game coming up and orders came down from the front office saying that the team was to leave Detroit on Saturday morning, Wilson would immediately schedule our departure for Friday afternoon. Things like that. It became obvious that the club and Wilson had to come to a parting of the ways.

George's departure came just before Christmas and it was handled in an awfully untidy manner. One morning, three of his assistant coaches—Bob Nussbaumer, Les Bingaman and Don Doll—were suddenly fired by owner Ford. A few days later, the remaining two—Aldo Forte and Sonny Grandelius—were also asked to leave. It was clear to everyone what the Detroit management was trying to do—get Wilson to resign. They had robbed him of his authority, humiliated him. He was absolutely crushed. Of course, he quit.

Within a week or so, Wilson caught on with the Redskins as an assistant coach. He stayed there for one season and then became head coach of the Miami Dolphins in the American Football League.

To replace George, the Lions brought in Harry Gilmer. I knew Gilmer because during the time I was with the Steelers, he was Buddy Parker's defensive coach. He had been an All American at Alabama and he had quarterbacked the team to victories in both the Sugar Bowl and Rose Bowl. Injuries hurt his pro career, but he played nine years, the last three of which were spent with the Lions. Before coming to the Lions as Wilson's successor, Gilmer had been an assistant to Norm Van Brocklin at Minnesota. I knew Van Brocklin worked his players hard. There would be a couple of three-quarter-speed scrimmages during the week and they usually resulted in some hard knocking. I wondered if Gilmer planned to follow this policy in Detroit. It was something we weren't used to.

Right at the beginning Gilmer made it clear he did not believe in the shuttle system for quarterbacks. "When you divide the job you divide the team," he said. It became obvious that either Milt or I would soon be asked to pack up and leave, and it didn't take me long to deduce that it wasn't to be Milt.

The previous season, after I had broken my collarbone, Milt took over as quarterback for the final eight games of the season. He was never better, surely because he knew I wasn't going to be warming up. By the end of the season, he was rated as the hottest passer in the league. Gilmer believed that he could do the same kind of job in 1965.

If Gilmer did have any doubts about letting me go, I probably resolved them during an exhibition game we played late in August against the Baltimore Colts. Played at night, it was the annual charities game of the Detroit *Free Press*. Tiger Stadium was jammed. It was my first starting assignment since I had broken my collarbone and I was rusty. I also think I may have tried too hard. I overthrew passes; I underthrew them. It was a gruesome night. I don't know when I ever heard so many boos. I completed only five of twenty-one passes, and netted only sixteen yards in the air. We lost, 23–2. When I ran off the field at the end to the unfriendly cries from the stands, the thought struck me that it was probably my last game in a Detroit uniform.

After that game, Gilmer hardly ever used me in practice again. The coaches seldom talked to me. It was like I had a contagious disease. Our next exhibition game was against the Browns, and I didn't play at all. After the game, Jane and I went out to dinner with some friends. We had just ordered when I got a phone call from Russ Thomas.

"I'm coming over to see you, Earl," he said. I knew something was up.

When Russ arrived, he took Jane and me aside and broke the news. They had worked out a deal sending me to the New York Giants. It was a complex arrangement. In exchange for me, the Lions got offensive guard Darrell Dess, an eight-year veteran and much valued player in New York, plus linebacker Mike Lucci, then beginning his fourth year, plus a future draft choice. Lucci had gone to the Giants from the Cleveland Browns in a "paper" trade just minutes before he was sent to the Lions. For Lucci, the Browns got defensive back Erich Barnes.

The news of the trade didn't make us happy. Thomas went on at great length about what a great opportunity it was, about how sorely New York needed a proven quarterback. I had heard all this before. It sounded like the same script Frankie Albert had used when the Forty-Niners shipped me to the Steelers.

It was a jolt. I had been playing in Detroit for seven years, and we had been living in the Detroit area for almost that long. My wife felt this was our home. It was going to be rough uprooting the family. Besides, I had an off-season job with a solid future. How was that going to be affected?

Any trade is tough to take. There's something lonely about being sent to another club. After all, your whole life is built around your team. When a player is sent to another club, his wife always says, "*We've* been traded." It's always "we."

Guys on the team are much more than just your teammates; they're your friends. And if you're playing in a strange city, they may be your only friends. You're very close to your teammates, much closer than you are to your co-workers if you're employed, say, as a salesman or an accountant or you're stamping out fenders at a Dodge plant.

After Vince Lombardi gave up coaching at the end of the 1967 season, he realized that he had made a horrible mistake. And during his brief retirement, do you know what he missed the most? It wasn't the high excitement of the games; it wasn't the thrill of winning, or the eminence, or the adulation. There is "a great closeness" on a football team, he once said, and that is what he missed. He felt a tremendous loss at not being able to share in the rapport that exists between a coach and his team.

I've often felt that a professional football team is something like a small fighting force, a band of men specially trained and equipped to make war upon a common enemy. And as with any fighting force, there develops a deep comradeship and warm congeniality among the members. When you're traded, all that's destroyed. It really hurts. You feel awfully desolate. I hate to be traded. Every player does.

The Giants were a young team and I only knew one player there—Jim Katcavage, an end. We had played together on the College All Star team in 1956.

But there was really no choice. I had to go. I had no

future with Detroit. Recent events had made that clear. And the Giants *did* need quarterbacking help. I wouldn't be warming the bench; there'd be no shuttle system. I was sure to be playing.

CHAPTER THIRTEEN

When Y. A. Tittle joined the Giants in 1961, his early days with the team were among the loneliest in his life. He was like a visitor from an unfriendly country. His teammates were aloof, even suspicious, at least at first, for Tittle was the man who was meant to replace Charlie Conerly, and Conerly was held in the highest esteem in New York; he was really something special.

But when I arrived at the Giants training camp at Fairfield University in Fairfield, Connecticut, I experienced no resentment, no animosity. Just the opposite, in fact. I was looked upon as a rescuer, as someone they hoped would deliver the team out of the bondage represented by last place in the league standings where the team had finished the year before.

Allie Sherman, the Giants coach, and I were on the same wavelength right from the start. We had long talks together, and he assured me that I was going to be the No. 1 quarterback. "I'm behind you one hundred per cent," he said. "Whatever you do out there, I'll back you up. Depend on it." Nothing like this had ever happened to me before. Everything looked great.

Maybe one reason Sherman and I hit it off so well was because he had been a quarterback, first at Brooklyn College and then, during the mid-1940's, with the Philadelphia Eagles. What's more he had been a backup quarterback, playing behind the Eagles' Tommy Thompson, a deadly passer. He knew well what it meant to sit on the bench. Sherman had become head coach of the Giants in 1960 following a year as offensive coach with the team, two years as a scout, and three years as head coach of Winnipeg in the Canadian league.

Sherman's strongest point was his profound knowledge of the game. Everyone agreed he had an excellent football mind. Plus he had an irrepressible enthusiasm for the game. At training camp, he tried to be everywhere at once and seemed to be involved with the minutest details. He was not big; indeed, he often looked out of place on the field. He was a sensitive guy. Barry Gottehrer, in recording the history of the New York Giants, referred to Sherman as a "proud emotionalist," an apt description. When you praised the team, he glowed. But criticism stung him.

Unfortunately, there was a lot to criticize. The Giants had just been through one of the worst seasons in the club's history, and the Giants have a very long history.

Sherman was under fire from the fans, the press, and there were even critical murmurings among the players. He had begun a drastic rebuilding program and many people said he had started too soon, trading away aging veterans before they were too aged. Gone were such favorites as Dick Modzelewski, Sam Huff and Phil King, all used as trade bait. Alex Webster, Frank Gifford and Andy Robustelli, other popular stars, had retired. Then the team got hit with some costly injuries. Y. A. Tittle was among those sidelined, and then he retired. Suddenly the Giants, champions for three consecutive years in the Eastern Conference—1961–1964—were foundering. In 1964, they finished dead last.

If the Giants situation in itself was not bad enough, the club was now in competition with the Jets for the attention and affection of New York fans. In fact, the AFL team was already beginning to overshadow its venerable rival. Early in 1965, Sonny Werblin, the Jets' owner at the time, signed a young All American quarterback from the University of Alabama by the name of Joe Namath. According to the press, Namath received a bonus of $400,000. Two weeks later Werblin signed John Huarte, an All American at Notre Dame. Huarte received a reported $200,000.

I was anxious to go to work, to learn the system. And to get to know the receivers. There's nothing more important for a quarterback. You have to know your receivers so thoroughly that you and they think exactly alike. Some receivers you can pick up right away. With others, it takes time, as much as a season or two or even more.

No two receivers go out the same way. Suppose I call a square-in pattern. This means that the receiver will break straight down the field eight to twelve yards, then cut to the inside at a ninety degree angle. Now the quarterback has to be able to tell by the receiver's actions precisely when he is going to make his cut. There'll be a little tip-off in the way he moves. It's hard to give an example of what I mean. It's slight; it's subtle, maybe only the wiggle movement of the shoulders or the hips. Suppose you see a man walk down a street day after day after day. Before long you don't have to see the man's face, yet you can tell with a quick glance who the man is. The distinguishing characteristics of his walk are what identify him. Well, when you're a quarterback, you have somewhat the same situation with your receivers. With one quick look, you have to be able to forecast what they're planning on doing.

Of course, knowing your receivers perfectly is only part of the job. A man can vary the way he runs a pattern for a multitude of reasons. He may be slow getting started; he may get held up in traffic. Take the simple sideline pass.

Some receivers like to run it almost as a square-out, breaking abruptly to the outside when they reach a point eight to ten yards beyond the line of scrimmage. Others go deeper than normal but hook back slightly as they near the sideline. Still others slant down, delaying their break until they're almost at the sideline. This type is tough to throw to. They take away the outside. Your timing has to be perfect.

One of the best receivers we had on the Giants was Joe Morrison. He had done everything for the club but give out the oranges at halftime. Sturdy—six-foot-one, 210—and indestructible. Morrison had played halfback, fullback, tight end and flanker at various times the year before. He had also played on the so-called suicide squads, the kickoff and punting teams. In his college days at Cincinnati, he played quarterback and later halfback. He signed with the Giants in 1959. Sherman made him a flanker the year I joined the team.

Joe had the strength to outfight most linebackers for the short pass and he almost always managed to get clear on the long ones. He had thick legs and took short choppy steps, and you knew he would never break any records with his speed, but he had surprising quickness and brilliant moves. He'd give a defenseman a head and shoulders dip, or start slow and put on a quick burst, and then the next time he might veer either to the right or left to get by. These are the types of moves a quarterback has to be able to recognize, and it's only by working with his receivers that he can gain this knowledge.

The Giants had another topflight pass catcher in Aaron Thomas. He had terrific speed and also good size and strength. He usually lined up at tight end, but in 1966, a year the club was hit hard with injuries, and Joe Morrison switched from being a flanker to a running back, Thomas took over Morrison's slot.

Then there was Homer Jones, a young man filling in for veteran Del Shofner who had been injured. I had never met any receiver quite like Homer. He played his college football at Texas Southern and had been with the Giants for two seasons, but he had failed to impress anybody and had been consigned to the taxi squad. Homer had blazing speed. He was as fast as any receiver I had ever thrown to. In fact, I'd rate him just about as fast as Bob Hayes of the Cowboys who has been tagged the "world's fastest human." This billing never impressed Homer much, and I've heard him say he could beat Hayes if he was pressed. I don't doubt it. He was once timed at 9.3 for the one hundred, and 20.3 for the 220, a distance at which he once actually did trim Hayes. Homer looked like a sprinter; he was tall—six-foot-two—and sort of spindly, but his legs were sturdy and well-muscled and he broke many a tackle to stretch a short gain into long distance.

Homer was so fast it was almost impossible to overthrow him on a fly pattern, but you could never be sure what was going to happen when he reached the ball. Once in a pre-game warmup he dropped nine consecutive passes, then in the game he caught a sixty-yarder. He had a really big pair of hands, and he could wrap his fingers around the ball the way most people clutch a grapefruit. I have thrown him hard bullets and seen him pluck them out of the air one-handed. But you never could be sure. Some guys called him the Question Mark.

In Homer's rookie year, defensemen really didn't realize what tremendous speed he had, and sometimes he'd run right by them. We connected on an awful lot of long passes. In the first game we played at Yankee Stadium, we faced the Eagles and we had just gotten a penalty, and I called Homer on a fly. I just reared back and hung the ball out there. It went sixty yards in the air. Homer, with his great speed, really turned it on, and he actually had to slow down to make the catch. When Irv Cross, the Eagles' safety man, tried to adjust his stride to match Homer's he stumbled. That's when Homer made the catch. He galloped into the end zone without anyone touching him. The play covered eighty-nine yards, the longest pass play in New York history.

Seldom, in the beginning, at least, would Homer stick to the pattern he was supposed to run. Suppose his assignment was to go down and break in. Well, if he saw the defenseman had taken away the inside, Homer wouldn't go in there. Or if he did go in, he'd just collide with the guy, just run right into him.

Sometimes Homer ran patterns that were his own creation. He once ran a seventy-five yard square out. Honest. He recognized no difference between a down-and-in and a down-and-out, at least in his first few games. A short slant could easily become a deep fly. More than once when we were going over the game films, Sherman would turn to end coach Ken Kavanaugh and ask, "Where the hell was Homer heading that time?" Kavanaugh would just shrug.

All Homer really wanted to do was run a fly, beat his man with sheer speed. "I got a play for you, Earl," he'd announce in the huddle, and I knew exactly what it was going to be—a deep pass to Homer. He really wasn't interested in the short stuff or any of the other patterns. After a while the other teams got to realize this and the defensemen assigned to Homer would be instructed to lay back ten or twelve yards and let Homer come to them. But

Homer still tried to beat the man with speed. Usually they'd be fifty or sixty yards out before Homer began to forge ahead and this meant that in order for me to lead Homer with the ball, I had to throw it eighty yards or so. Well, you know how many eighty yard pass plays there are each season. Eventually, Homer decided he'd learn some other patterns, too.

Homer was a good blocker in his first year with the club. At six-foot-two, 215, he surely had the size to be a blocker. But in time he became so absorbed in developing his skills as a receiver, he began to disregard his blocking assignments.

Once in a game against the Cardinals, I called a pass play that had me rolling out to the weak side. Homer was supposed to block the linebacker before going out. But when he lined up, I could see that Homer was nowhere near the linebacker, and the guy came blazing in. Homer raced into the end zone and somehow I got the ball to him and we had a touchdown.

The Giants of 1965 were a very young team. The squad included eleven rookies and eleven second year men. Gary Wood, the No. 2 quarterback, was in his second pro season. In 1964 he had been the backup man to Y. A. Tittle and took over for him late in the season after Y. A. had been injured. Gary was quick, smart and gutsy, but his problem was height, or lack of it. At five-foot-ten he had trouble passing the ball over the upstretched arms of the six-foot-four linemen. As a result he often had to rollout to get the ball away, not a practice I'd ever recommend. The Giants also had Bob Timberlake, another rollout thrower, and a very likable young man, but who lacked in quarterbacking experience.

While the club's greatest strength was their receiving corps, Sherman intended to rely on a heavy diet of running. The running backs personified Sherman's youth movement. We had Steve Thurlow and Ernie Wheelwright, both second year men, and two newcomers, Tucker Frederickson, the club's No. 1 draft pick, and Ernie Koy from the University of Texas.

We really could have used a placekicker. Sherman tried three or four different men, none of whom could even be called mediocre. One of them was Bob Timberlake. Once during the season Timberlake attended a banquet and afterward he held a question and answer session. Someone got up and said, "Bob, I don't want to say anything about your ability as field goal kicker, but I sure want to congratulate you for bringing the excitement back into the extra point play."

It was during this period that the Washington Redskins signed placekicker Charlie Gogolak for a bonus reported to be $300,000. "If Charlie Gogolak's foot is worth $300,000," someone once said to Timberlake in the locker room, "then your foot must be worth a $1.98."

My first appearance for New York came in an exhibition game just a few days after I arrived in camp. We played, of all teams, the Lions. The game was one-half of the spectacular football doubleheader that Cleveland owner Art Modell promotes each year, and 83,118 fans turned out, the largest pro crowd of the year. Sherman kept our offense simple, limiting the number and complexity of the plays.

The game began on a sour note. In the first quarter, I went back to pass and Sam Williams came blasting in. I tried to duck but his hand hooked my shoulder pad and he dragged me over backward and the ball squirted out of my hands. Darris McCord recovered for the Lions on our 6 yard line and three plays later they scored. The next time we got the ball I was smothered in the end zone by Williams and Karras for a safety. We were down, 11–0, at the half.

But in the third period the pass blocking improved and we scored three times, once on an eighty-two yard pass play with Aaron Thomas on the receiving end. Detroit came back with a pair of touchdowns to take a 25–21 lead and set the stage for a final effort on our part. In the dying minutes of the game, Dick Lynch recovered a fumble on the Lions' 22. When play resumed, there was time for only one sequence of downs. Three passes went incomplete. Then I called a slant to Homer Jones. He got clear; no one was within five yards of him. The pass was perfect—but it slithered through Homer's hands just as he crossed the goal line.

We should have beaten them. I sure would have liked to.

One thing I remember about the game was a battle of wits that I had with Joe Schmidt, one in which I came out very much the loser. On a first down situation I called a trap play, with the back running straight at Schmidt, the Lions middle linebacker, head on. Schmidt read the play perfectly and stopped the play right at the line of scrimmage. "He won't do that again," I figured, and I called the same play a second time and Schmidt read it again and was waiting. This time the runner got about a yard and now it was third and nine. "He's gotta be looking for the pass," I thought to myself. "He's gotta back up and get out of there. We'll cross him up with a run." And I called the exact same play. Schmidt wasn't fooled for a second and he stepped up and made the tackle a third time. We got two yards at the most. As I turned to run off the field, I caught a glimpse of Schmidt and he was still on the ground but he had propped himself up on one elbow and was shaking his fist at me and yelling, "Earl, you sonavabitch, quit running those traps; quit picking on me!"

After the game I happened to run into Allie Sherman at the hotel where the team was staying. He was in high spirits.

"You were great out there," he exclaimed, and he put his arm around my shoulder. "We should have won it."

"You've been in the league a long time," he said, "but you've never been with a winner. I'll bet you'd really like to play for a championship team. You must have a big desire for that."

I said I sure did.

"Well," said Allie, "we're going to have a championship club and you're going to be the guy who quarterbacks it."

You know, I believed him.

The team started poorly. We met the Cowboys in Dallas and I don't think we did a single thing right all day long. We came out of it badly mauled.

Philadelphia was next. We moved the ball well, but didn't score enough, and the Eagles led, 14–13, in the final minutes. Then from our own 20 yard line, I brought the team to the Philadelphia 5 in just two plays. Andy Stynchula came in and booted a field goal with eleven seconds remaining to give us a 16–14 win. It was a big game for me and a big one for the team. We really needed that win. The more you lose the more you're likely to lose. It becomes a habit. We proved we could win. We proved we could come through in the clutch. And all of this is doubly important when you have a young team.

One other game that year was especially significant. It was about the middle of the season and we were playing the St. Louis Cardinals. We were behind, 10-0, at the half. We got a touchdown in the third quarter and in the fourth quarter were driving for another with the ball on the Cards' 25. St. Louis was blitzing like crazy on almost every play. I called a deep pattern to Aaron Thomas and kept all the backs in to give me maximum protection. The Cards red-dogged again but no one touched me. Aaron broke into the clear and I hit him with a perfect pass just as he crossed the goal line. But he dropped the ball.

In the huddle, I called exactly the same play a second time. I saw Jerry Stovall, the Cardinals' left safety man, stop as Aaron kept on running. Stovall didn't think I would go to Thomas again, so stayed short, trying to pick up one of the backs. When Aaron crossed the goal line, he was all by himself, and he just turned around and waited for the ball. It was simple. We won the game on that play.

In Detroit I never would have considered using a play that misfired a second time. If I missed with it, I knew I'd be sitting down. But in New York I could gamble, and it made a big difference.

Our biggest problems that season were Cleveland and Jimmy Brown. We played the Browns twice and each time Jimmy was devastating. In our second meeting, he had one of his fantastic days, gaining 156 yards on the ground and catching three passes for thirty-six yards. We were not in the same class with Cleveland.

We came down to the end of the season with a 7–6 record. Dallas was 6–7 and we played them in the final game, one that would decide which team would go to the Playoff Bowl, the game held each year in Miami between the runners-up in the NFL's Eastern and Western Conferences. Playing in the Playoff Bowl has little significance—I've heard players refer to it as the Rotten Bowl—but it's something to look forward to because it means an expense-paid week in Miami in January. Sid Moret, one of our trainers, put up travel posters around the locker room, showing lush Florida scenes. Before the game with Washington the previous week, he had hung up a sign that said: TWO-FOR-TWO FOR THE FONTAINEBLEAU. Then after we beat the Redskins, he replaced it with one that proclaimed: ONE-FOR-ONE FOR MIAMI A GO-GO.

We kicked off and the Cowboys promptly drove to our 1 yard line and then lost the ball on a fumble. We were forced to punt and Dallas came right back, but we made them settle for a field goal.

Late in the first quarter Dallas scored on a sixty-five-yarder from Don Meredith to Bob Hayes who outran Dick Lynch to the end zone. Meanwhile, I was having problems. The Cowboys were blitzing a lot and I spent a great deal of time on my back looking at the sky. Besides, I wasn't having one of my better passing days. I wasn't hitting consistently. I had men open but I missed. We didn't get on the scoreboard until the second quarter when I connected with Aaron Thomas for a touchdown. Dallas got it right back, however, on another Meredith to Hayes pass to make it 17–17 at the half.

In the third quarter we began with a rush, moving sixty yards after the kickoff and I ended the drive with a toss to Bob Crespino in the end zone. We had the momentum now. I felt sure we were going to go all the way. Then came a play that broke our back. Just before the fourth quarter began, we drove to the Dallas 35 yard line and there the Cowboys held. Jerry Hillebrand, who had taken over the role of the team's placekicker, came in to try one. Jerry booted, but Cornell Green, rushing in, sprang high into the air to block it. Obert Logan grabbed up the ball and sprinted sixty yards for the touchdown. This killed us. Instead of it being a tie game, we were now behind, 24–14.

After the kickoff, we brought the ball down the field once more and I hit Crespino again for a touchdown. Andy Stynchula came in to kick the extra point and *that* was blocked. We needed that point to get within field goal range of the Cowboys and when we didn't get it whatever remained of the team's confidence oozed away. The final score read: Dallas, 38; New York, 20. Mercifully, Sid Moret had removed the Florida travel posters by the time we got back to the locker room.

It had been a rugged season but a good one. Everyone from Well Mara on down was satisfied with the fact we finished in a tie for second place and a 7–7 record. We had done better, much better, than any one had figured, and with a field goal kicker we might easily have won another game or two.

More than once the team beat itself. There were games in which the offensive line disintegrated. There were games in which defense took the day off. But this always happens when you have rookies in key spots, when you're reconstructing a team.

I threw twenty-two touchdown passes for the season, five more than the Giant total in 1964. I was intercepted only nine times, and the season before the Giants had had twenty-five passes picked off. It was one of my best season's as a pro. The team voted me their most valuable player trophy.

"You can't give enough credit to Morrall," Sherman told the press. "He did a helluva job for us." I could hardly wait for 1966.

CHAPTER FOURTEEN

When I was with the Giants, one of my best friends was Tucker Frederickson. And he still is.

He was a rookie in 1965, the year I joined the club. Few players have come into the NFL with greater fanfare. He was an All American at Auburn where he did everything but put down the chalk lines, and during his senior year he led the team in rushing, pass receiving, and scoring. He was named Player of the Year in the South and Most Valuable Player in the Southeastern Conference. One NFL scout said of him: "He can go in the first round of the draft in any one of five different positions—running back, tight end, fullback, cornerback or safety." He was the Giants' first draft choice that year and the club by-passed Joe Namath to get him. It was reported that he received $125,000 for signing.

Not overly big, Tucker stood six-foot-two and weighed about 225, but he had remarkable strength in his arms and legs. He was a kidder and extremely popular with the guys on the team. He had style, poise and a boyish handsomeness. He was everyone's conception of what a football hero should look like. He was the Goldenboy.

Allie Sherman saw Tucker strictly as a running back and it's not hard to understand why. While he didn't have great speed or an array of fancy moves, Tucker had a perfect understanding of the game, an instinctive feel of where the hole was going to be. He was always sliding toward the crack, and if there was no opening he'd put his head down and blast right in there. He wasn't afraid.

He'd stick his nose in. If he got hurt, you never knew it. Even in his rookie year, you could always count on him for yardage. He never hurt you, never picked the wrong hole. He got the most out of every situation. He was a fine pass receiver, too, and always managed to get out where you wanted him.

I remember a game late in Tucker's rookie season. We were playing the Steelers and were behind in the second quarter, 10–7. I completed a pass to Del Shofner for forty-one yards that got us deep into Pittsburgh territory. Not long after, I handed off to Tuck from thirteen yards out and he turned left end, then made a great move on Jimmy Bradshaw, the Steelers' safety, and swept into the end zone. Nobody even touched him.

We recovered a fumble on the Steelers' 9 yard line right after the kickoff, and I passed to Tucker and he scored a second time. Soon after, the Steelers fumbled again, this time on a punt attempt, and we took over on their 19. I shot a little flare to Tucker and he grabbed it and took off. Bradshaw hit him at the 5, but Tucker kept going. Then Brady Keys piled into him at the 2. Still Tucker wouldn't go down, and when he crossed the goal line both guys were hanging on to him.

He had scored three touchdowns in three and a half minutes. Now we were leading 28–10. Having Tucker on your team was like having an extra man or two.

Tucker played every game but one in 1965 and was a key factor in the modest success the club enjoyed; I mean our second-place finish. He wound up with 659 yards gained rushing; he was on the receiving end of twenty-four passes, and there wasn't a better blocker in the league. He was named New York's Rookie of the Year and one newspaperman called him the "best Giant back of all time."

With his on-the-field success came the autograph sessions, speaking engagements and endorsements. He became a registered representative with a Wall Street brokerage firm, and later joined Allen & Co., an investment banking house.

At training camp at Fairfield late the next summer, the bubble burst. It happened during a nutcracker, a simple but violent drill that involves eight players—a center, two defensive linemen, two on offense, a quarterback and two halfbacks. The quarterback hands to one of his running backs who cuts off blocking into the line, hopefully into a gap that's been created. "Nutcracker" is a very appropriate name.

On this play, I took the snap, turned and handed to Tucker. He cut sharply to his right, but there was no opening, only a tangle of bodies. Jeff Smith, a 240-pound linebacker, got an arm around Tucker's ankles but couldn't bring him down. As Tucker wriggled to get free, Rosey Davis, a 260-pound defensive end, roared in from the side and hit like a fast bus and Tucker crumpled to the ground, his left knee buckling to the side.

Right away you knew it was bad. Tucker grabbed his leg, his head went back and his face showed the pain. "It's all right, Tuck; it's all right. Don't worry. You're going to be O. K." We said all the lies as we helped him from the field.

Dr. Anthony Pisani, the club doctor and an orthopedic specialist, arrived later in the day and, after examining Tucker, said that no serious damage had been done. Surgery wouldn't be necessary. The knee, he felt, would heal by itself. But Tucker never shared the doctor's optimism. "It just doesn't feel right," he said. "I just can't believe it's going to be O. K."

Tucker did special exercises to strengthen the muscles of the injured leg, took whirlpool baths and within a week or so he was running again. Early in September, just before our first preseason game, Tucker seemed to be in good shape. Yet he was lacking in confidence. It was almost as if he expected something to happen.

We played Green Bay and Sherman started him. Early in the first quarter, I went back to pass and was rushed. Tucker, out on the flat, was my safety valve. No one was near him. He had to cut back to get the ball and when he pivoted the knee gave way. This time he was carried from the field. You knew it had to be serious—and it was, very serious.

I never—thank God—have suffered a knee injury. I've had some sore knees, probably resulting from the ligaments being stretched, but any problems I've had have been quite minor. Quarterbacks are the most likely victims of knee injuries, especially the scramblers. But every quarterback puts himself in jeopardy whenever he drops back, sets and then starts to search for a receiver. He never thinks about protecting himself. His mind is on the play, on getting the pass off.

During 1966, the year that Tucker was hurt, two quarterbacks—Bill Wade of the Bears, and Charley Johnson of the Cardinals—were put out of action by knee injuries. Joe Namath's knees have gotten more newspaper space than his right arm. Obviously, the knee wasn't built for quarterbacking, or, indeed, for football.

Knee injuries differ widely as to type and degree of seriousness. Sometimes the injury concerns only the cartilage, the two small pads of tough elastic tissue between the two large bones of the leg, the thigh bone (the femur) and the shin bone (the fibia). A player can sustain cartilage damage in a pile-up, by being clipped, or by being blocked, particularly from the blind-side. The cartilage tears or frays, then sometimes rolls up into a tight ball. The result is loss of mobility in the leg and constant pain. When knee trouble is suspected, doctors inject air and dye into the joint, then x-ray it. To repair cartilage damage, the surgeon makes a diagonal incision on the side of the knee cap to expose the joint, then cuts away the pad of cartilage. After the operation, the space fills naturally with air and fluid. The pain disappears and the player regains most of his mobility. The repair or removal of cartilage, while not exactly routine, is fairly common nowadays, and it is a matter of regrettable fact that there are more knee scars than players in the locker room of any given pro team. Some players, of course, have never had to undergo knee surgery, but most have, and sometimes on both knees and occasionally two or three times on the same knee. Dr. Pisani performed ten or eleven knee operations one season I was with the Giants.

More serious than a cartilage problem is damage to the bone and the shin bone. The medial ligament is on the inside of the knee, and the lateral ligament is on the outside. The two others—the cruciate ligaments—crisscross from front to back.

Imagine a quarterback dropping back to pass. Before he fires, he plants his right foot firmly. Suppose he's grabbed hip high and his body wrenched to the right or left. If the cleats aren't wrested free, the thigh bone turns but the shin bone doesn't. Something has to give; it may be one or more of the ligaments. They pull or tear and the result,

112

besides the pain, is a wobbly knee. In the case of injury to the medial and lateral ligaments, the player can sit on the edge of a high table dangling his legs, and he can waggle the lower part of the injured limb from side to side by as much as an inch or more while keeping the thigh perfectly still.

In cases where there is damage to the cruciate ligaments, there is back and forth "play" in the lower leg. Imagine you're sitting on the floor, your legs stretched out. Imagine being able to take hold of your lower leg and lift it straight up a couple of inches while your upper leg remains flat on the floor. I know more than one player who can do that.

Most doctors work fast to repair ligament damage, especially in the case of a tear, because the torn ends deteriorate quickly, becoming soft and thus making repair work difficult. If the ligament has been stretched, the surgeon doubles it back on itself, then stitches a pleat with sutures. If there's a tear, the two ends are overlapped and then stitched together. The cruciate ligaments, because they lie deep within the joints, are the most difficult to repair.

Gil Mains, once a tackle for the Lions, and now a neighbor of mine in Bloomfield Hills, was once blocked on the blind side on a kickoff play during a game against the Forty-Niners, and the ligaments on both sides of one knee were torn away. Doctors grafted them together again, but today Gil walks with a limp and the knee gives him a lot of pain. Doctors now want to fuse the joint. His kneecap, as George Plimpton described it in *Paper Lion,* is as "shapeless and large in his leg as if two or three large handfuls of socks were sewn in there."

Following an operation involving ligaments, the player

usually has to spend four to six weeks with the leg in a heavy cast. Months of exercises follow. At first they are extremely painful. Weights are attached to the foot of the injured leg, and the man has to lift them, sometimes with the knee bent, other times with the leg extended. The idea, of course, is to rebuild the muscles to make the injured leg at least as strong as the other.

The recuperative period is unfailingly grim, for there is always the knowledge that the whole thing might be futile. Some players respond to the treatment and are playing fulltime again a year or so after the surgery. John Henry Johnson of the Steelers and Greg Larson of the Giants are two examples of players who bounced back without any apparent loss of skill. E. J. Holub of the Kansas City Chiefs has had several knee operations—all the crimson lines on his knees, someone once told me, give the appearance of a road map—but this hasn't prevented him from carving out an outstanding career as a center and linebacker. But many players never come back. You hardly ever hear of them. When they leave, they don't even get a paragraph on the sports page.

All manner of suggestions have been put forth in an effort to prevent knee injuries. The cleatless heel is one. You can wear a knee brace for protection, but it cuts down your mobility. Artificial turf may be part of the answer, or shorter cleats. Or both. Some team doctors recommend special exercises to strengthen the muscle structure of the knee. During the off-season, I play handball two or three times a week and this helps to condition my legs. No one seems close to a solution, however. During the 1968 season, Gale Sayers, the Bears' brilliant running back, and quarterback Jack Kemp of the Buffalo Bills, both suffered torn knee ligaments.

I think a primary reason for the increased number of knee injuries is the fact that players today are bigger and faster than ever before. It's a case of a larger mass traveling at a greater speed. When they hit, they hit hard and something has to give. Because it happens to be the weakest link, it's the knee.

Tucker Frederickson's knee injury was especially serious. He had torn both a cruciate and medial ligament and damaged the cartilage. The whole knee had to be rebuilt. A nine-inch incision was cut, and holes were drilled in the leg bones above and below the knee. Then muscle tissue was taken from the back of his thigh and new ligaments created from it, and these were sewn through the holes to bind the leg.

I visited Tucker in the hospital. He was able to smile, although I'm sure it was the most agonizing experience of his young life. He seemed to have resigned himself to the long, grim struggle ahead.

He spent weeks in a cast, hobbling about on crutches, and the muscles in the once powerful leg atrophied and the limb's girth began to shrink. His weight fell by twenty pounds. Toward the end of the season, Tucker began to walk again and even to run easily. He was with the team for every game. While we dressed and were taped, he sat on an equipment trunk and watched silently, hardly moving. During the game he was on the bench, but dressed in street clothes. Sometimes he helped out on the phones, but usually he was a lone and almost forgotten figure.

When the season ended and the other players headed home, Tucker stayed in New York to continue his reconditioning program. He'd report each day to trainer Johnny Dziegel at the therapy room at Yankee Stadium. He worked out on a bicycle exerciser and used the various types of special weight-lifting equipment. He ran endlessly—around the red gravel track that encircles the playing field and up and down the steep concrete staircases in the empty upper deck. It was a long, wearying winter. If success depended on determination, Tucker would be in the Hall of Fame.

By March, Tucker's weight and strength were back to normal and he played basketball and found that he had regained his speed and mobility. But he was troubled because the knee didn't feel right. It had a jiggle in it, a looseness. "Don't worry," trainer Johnny Dziegel told him. "It's normal. You're going to be O.K."

Just about everyone on the team shared Dziegel's optimism. I know I did. I wasn't as nearly concerned about the knee's ability to restore itself as I was about Tucker's mental attitude.

In the early games the next season, Tucker seemed to lack something, his courage or his daring. But little by little you could see him improve. Then, as he was approaching his former brilliance, it happened again. The Giants were playing the Steelers and it was late in the first period. Tucker, running a slant, found his hole and got a first down. But in the pileup that followed the tackle, someone slammed into his extended right leg. Tucker knew he'd been hurt, but he limped back into the huddle and carried the ball on the very next play. But that was it. When he hobbled off the field, the trainers were waiting for him. The other knee had gone. Then came the surgery, the long period of recuperation, and all the anxiety.

But Tucker came back the next season and again the

next. How long he'll keep coming back, no one knows. He says he couldn't possibly endure the ordeal of another comeback. But I wonder. Tucker is like all the rest of us. There's something about this game that really gets you. It's very tough to quit.

CHAPTER FIFTEEN

The idea of finishing second again did not appeal to Sherman. Three times he had led the Giants to the Eastern Conference Championship—in 1961, 1962, and 1963. Twice he had been named Coach of the Year—in 1961 and 1962. He knew what it meant to be on top and he liked it there. "There are better things than seven and seven," he said more than once during training camp in 1966. "You wanna shoot for the whole thing."

But there were frightful problems. Defense was the chief one. The only regular returning to the defensive line was end Jim Katcavage. The other spots were filled by rookies or players shifted from other positions.

Everywhere you looked you saw a new face. And something was missing, the closeness, the spark a team needs. You could feel it. Allie, depite his high hopes, seemed to realize that something was wrong. He was much more frenetic than usual, driving himself and his coaches to the breaking point.

Then the amiable relationship that Allie and I had enjoyed began to warp. I think the turning point came one afternoon at Fairfield. We were having a two-minute drill, a session devoted to various plays the team might utilize during the final two minutes of a half. It was late in the day after a hard morning scrimmage and a long afternoon and it was hot. We were dirty and we were tired. But Allie and his coaches were running about frantically keeping everyone busy and worked up.

Three coaches were involved at our end of the field, and

one was supposed to yell out the situation—the down and yardage we had to make—and then I'd call a play to fit and we'd run it. Well, on this particular play, each one of the three coaches gave different instructions. "Second and nine," one of them yelled. "Third and two," called another. "Third and eleven," said the third one. That's how screwed-up things were. I didn't know what was going on. Finally we got together and straightened it out. It was to be third and eleven.

Just as I stepped into the huddle to call the play, I heard Allie scream at me, his voice several decibels higher than usual. "Cut out wasting time. Get moving. Call that ——— play."

This really burned me. Here he was bawling me out and he'd got the whole place looking like a scene out of a Jerry Lewis movie. I yelled right back. "Why don't you get things straightened out, then maybe I *can* call something."

As soon as the words were out, I knew I had made a mistake. Allie is supreme. He does not like to see his authority questioned. I saw his lips tighten. I saw his face go white. I bent into the huddle to call the play. Suddenly Allie was there. "Don't ever talk back to me," he said, and the words came slowly and deliberately and you could feel the heat. "Don't ever," he said. "I'm running this show. Remember that." Then he left.

Not long after this incident, another flare-up took place. We were playing a pre-season game in Nashville against the Falcons. We were leading, 7–0, and the game was in its early stages. I went back to pass and I found my primary receiver covered, so I unloaded to another man. It was a bad pass; it was late and in back of the intended receiver. A defensive player picked it off and went for a touchdown.

As I came off the field, I could see Allie waiting. He was boiling.

"How the hell could you do that?" he screamed. "You're ruining my team!"

"Don't worry, Allie," was about all I said. Sure, I had botched up the play. I didn't need Sherman to tell me that. But he kept it up. For fully five minutes, he stormed up and down in front of the bench, and he kept repeating, "I'm not going to let you ruin my team."

"Where does he get that 'my team' stuff?" I thought to myself. "It's *my* team, too."

Well, we went on to win the game, 14—7. But my relationship with Sherman was hardly chummy after that.

It was easy to understand the reasons for Sherman's temperamental outbursts. The Giants of 1966 were a horror. The youthful players lacked poise and assurance, while the handful of veterans were wary. Tucker's loss was a heavy psychological blow, and it worsened things considerably. A great pall of uncertainty hung over the club. We knew something awful was going to happen, but yet we hoped we were wrong.

Our worst fears were confirmed before the season was two hours old. We played Pittsburgh in the opening game and we were flat and careless, but still managed to get a tie, 34—34.

The game had one bright note. It came in the fourth quarter. It was first down and we had the ball on our 2 yard line. We were behind, 31—20, and I knew I had to gamble, so I called a fly pattern to Homer. At the snap, Homer broke straight downfield like he had been shot from a cannon. He didn't fake, didn't look to the left or right, just ran. I was about ten yards into the end zone when

I threw and I really gave it a shot. I thought I might have overthrown him.

After I fired, players in front of me on the field blocked off my view of Homer. We were playing at Pitt Stadium and when I went back to pass, there was this high-pitched roar of excitement, and it got louder when I put the ball in the air, then—bang—it stopped. I knew then that Homer had made the catch. The films showed the ball traveled about sixty-five yards in the air. Homer, who had his man beaten by a couple of steps, just ran under the ball grabbed it and then sprinted into the end zone.

In the NFL record book, the play gets a line of type that reads: "Earl Morrall (to Jones), N.Y. vs. Pitts., Sept. 11, 1966, 98 yards." At the time, it ranked as the second longest pass completion in league history.

The next week we got smothered by the Cowboys, 52–7. Then we lost in succession to Philadelphia, Cleveland and St. Louis. We finally won a game, beating Washington.

There were many things wrong with the team. I've already mentioned the defense. They were weak in pass blocking and, incredible as it may seem, there was virtually no pass rush. The offensive line was easily punctured. In a game against the Eagles, I was dropped five times in the first half. I was flattened once in a game against Washington and had trouble remembering my name for the rest of the day. The team moved aimlessly from one bleak Sunday afternoon to the next. There was no pride, no spirit, no confidence. I had never experienced anything like it. It made me sick.

This was a Saturday and we were scheduled to play the Cardinals at Yankee Stadium the next day and we were having a light workout, merely running through some of our goal line plays. On the next to last play of the day, I called a short pass, a play that involved a fake to Allen Jacobs, one of our running backs. Ordinarily, when I fake a handoff, I use the football. I put it right out there. That's standard. But this time—why, I'll never know—I just put out my empty right hand, while holding the ball to my belly with the left. Jacobs, running hard, brought up his elbow as he came by and it struck me square on the tip of the thumb, jamming the thumb so that the wrist took the full impact of the blow. The pain was bad. It felt like an electric shock. I shook the hand a few times and said a few choice words. Gary Wood finished the practice.

There was this deep pain in the wrist as I came off the field and it was beginning to swell. Johnny Johnson, the trainer, looked at it and said I'd better get some x-rays right away.

"I'll be O.K. Just put some tape on it," I said.

"No. I'm calling the doctor."

The next morning I got the news. I had cracked a bone in the wrist. "You can't play today," Dr. Pisani, the team doctor told me. "But it's not bad. You should be all right by next week."

Well, I wasn't. They put a small cast on the wrist, no bigger than a wristband, giving me almost total use of my right hand. But whenever I tried to throw the ball I got this terrific pain. I couldn't get any distance at all and my short passes didn't have any zip. I was beginning to get worried.

Gary Wood took over as quarterback and then, to back him up, the club brought up Tom Kennedy from the Brooklyn Dodgers of the Continental League.

Another week went by and I showed no improvement. They kept taking x-rays. Then Dr. Pisani finally found the source of the trouble. A second bone in the wrist was also cracked, a small flat bone called the carpal navicular. Carpal, someone told me, means pertaining to the wrist; navicular means boat-shaped. The bone had a hairline crack through the center.

After this discovery, I talked at length with Dr. Pisani and he really got me worried. In many cases, he explained, a break of this type never heals, and surgery has to be performed to remove the decaying bone chips. And once the bone is out, of course, the patient's hand movement becomes restricted. This is a helluva injury for a quarterback to have, and when I came out of that meeting with Dr. Pisani, I was really down. Not only was I upset by the thought that I might never throw a football again, but I was wondering whether I would have normal use of my hand, whether I'd be able to sign my name or stir my morning coffee. Dr. Pisani's gloom about my future was relayed to Sherman and Mara. My career was taking an abrupt turn.

As it was explained to me, the problem with my wrist was that only about one-half of the cracked bone was getting a supply of blood, the half that was linked into the vascular system. To get blood to the other half, Dr. Pisani wanted to perform a bone graft, a procedure that involves drilling a tiny hole in each side of the bone, then inserting a bone pin to connect the two halves. This bridges the gap across the fracture permitting blood to flow. But medical opinion differs as to whether this is a practical form of treatment. I told Dr. Pisani that since we had already waited a month or so, I'd like to have some more time to decide whether to go ahead with the surgery.

I went back to Detroit and talked to the doctors at Ford Hospital who had treated me in 1964 when I had broken

123

my collarbone. A Dr. David Mitchell, Sr., there really impressed me. "Let's let nature take a crack at it first," he advised. "If the bone doesn't heal by itself, then we'll operate." I decided to follow this more conservative course and Dr. Pisani and Sherman gave their approval. Dr. Mitchell encased the arm in a cast that extended from the elbow to the base of the fingers, completely immobilizing my hand. I wore the cast for four months, a very long four months.

When I returned to the Giants, things were very different. Sherman hardly noticed me. The same with the other coaches. The Giants had written me off. I knew it. They felt I was washed up.

When things were going well, when you were making a meaningful contribution to team victories, Sherman loved you. You got the hugs and kisses—actually. But when you ceased to contribute, no matter the reason, Sherman closed you out of his world. It was as if he had a list of players on the squad, and when you could no longer help he simply scratched your name off the list. And once this happened, well, you'd better have had something else going for you, because you were never going to make it with the New York Giants. In my case, of course, there were extenuating circumstances; I mean my wrist. But I remember in 1965 when I first joined the team and we'd have a scrimmage, Sherman always seemed to be down on certain players, and these guys were needled constantly. Even the smallest error was the cause for criticism. Frank Lasky, an offensive tackle who had been with the team the season before, was one player who had been crossed off Sherman's list. Linebacker John Carroll, a rookie from Notre Dame, was another. The 1965 season was Lasky's last, and Carroll was sent to the Redskins in 1966. You knew it was coming.

The Giants had two powerful and very promising running backs in Ernie Wheelwright and Steve Thurlow. Both had joined the club in 1964, and both were under continual harassment from Sherman, Thurlow especially. Even though Thurlow played good ball through most of 1965, Sherman was on him about his weight. Steve was a happy-go-lucky guy and he'd just shrug his shoulders. And this infuriated Allie all the more. In 1966 he traded Thurlow to Washington. The same year Sherman shipped Wheelright to the Atlanta Falcons. Wheelwright was a man Sherman once described as "the most powerful runner we have had in all my years with the Giants."

After I fractured my wrist, I spent the balance of the season watching from the bench. I do not remember anything pleasant happening.

We lost to the Rams, 55–14, as Los Angeles racked up thirty-eight first downs, an NFL record, and gained 572 yards on offense. We lost to the Falcons; it was their first win ever in the NFL. It is difficult to choose the team's worst performance that year, but it might have come one afternoon when we lost to Washington, 72–41.

We ended with a 1–12–1 record and were judged to be the poorest team in Giant history. We also ranked as the most-scored-upon team in the forty-six years of the NFL. We gave up 501 points.

I remember the final game. It was played at Yankee Stadium on a dark afternoon and we lost to Dallas, 17–7. There were always anti-Sherman banners displayed in the stands but this day there seemed to be more than ever before, and the singing of "Good-bye, Allie," a song that had been No. 1 on the fans' hit parade for a number of seasons, had unusual fervor. As the gun went off signaling the end of the game and the woeful season, a cordon of police surrounded Allie and escorted him to safety.

I couldn't help but think how terribly premature all the farewells were. Allie at the time was completing his second year on a remarkable ten year contract. And if anyone was going to be leaving, it was me.

Gary Cuozzo at Baltimore, who played behind Unitas, and George Mira at San Francisco, the backup man to John Brodie, were both unhappy with their second-string status and looking for greener pastures. The Giants were supposed to be very interested in drafting either Steve Spurrier of the University of Florida or Bob Griese of Purdue. And hardly a week went by that some newspaper didn't report that Fran Tarkenton, the quarterback at Minnesota, who had been feuding with his boss, coach Norm Van Brocklin, wasn't heading for New York.

"What's this all about?" I asked Allie one day not long before the season ended. "Are you trying to get Tarkenton?"

"Hell, no. Don't pay any attention to those rumors. You're going to be our quarterback next year. We're counting on you coming back."

"Good," I said, "because I'm counting on it, too."

CHAPTER SIXTEEN

Of course, the Giants did make the deal for Tarkenton. I got the news from Well Mara the morning the trade was made. It was a nice gesture, his calling me. One good thing about the Giants was the warm relationship that existed between the players and the club's top officials, Mara and Ray Walsh, the general manager.

Ironically, Mara's call came just about two weeks after the cast had been removed from my wrist. I had begun a rigorous program to rebuild the arm and the results were beginning to show already. I had full use of the wrist and there was little pain. I was very hopeful. Then the door was slammed.

One official with the Giants organization described Tarkenton as the "most expensive player" the club had ever got. Indeed, they paid a heavy price for him, giving up their first and second draft choices in 1967, plus their first draft choice in 1968, plus another player to be named later.

I wouldn't have minded competing with Tarkenton for the No. 1 job, but I never got the opportunity. Sherman made that clear. He just handed the job to Tarkenton. "We needed a top quarterback," he told the press when announcing the trade, "and Tarkenton is a top quarterback." The job was Tarkenton's. It had to be that way. After all, Sherman had mortgaged the team's future to get Frank. How would it look if he now made Tarkenton a benchsitter? He couldn't do it. He'd be telling everyone he made a bad deal.

I like Tarkenton. He's the son of a Methodist minister and a member of the Fellowship of Christian Athletes. He played his college football at the University of Georgia. He's friendly and personable. He's got intelligence, poise, and guts.

Tarkenton's teacher was Norm Van Brocklin, one of pro football's all-time great quarterbacks and coach of the Vikings when Fran joined the team. Actually, Tarkenton's schooling began well before he even graduated. Van Brocklin sent him an NFL football in the spring. "Get used to throwing and handling it," he said. "It's different from the college ball." (It's bigger around the middle.) Tarkenton was expected to understudy veteran George Shaw during his rookie year, but he developed so quickly that Van Brocklin made him the Vikings' starting quarterback his very first season. That was 1961.

In his career with the Rams and the Eagles, Van Brocklin was strictly a drop-back quarterback, a pocket passer. But Tarkenton became a scrambler—indeed, the prince of scramblers. When trapped by pass rushers, he would dart about like a frightened squirrel, not to gain yardage necessarily, but time, time for his receivers to get clear and time to get the pass off.

The Minnesota defenses were sievelike in those days, so Fran's scrambling style was born partly out of desperation. Also, he's an inch or so shorter than the average quarterback (he's listed as being six feet, but I don't think he's quite that tall), so when he remains in the pocket, his view of his receivers is often blocked and it's also difficult for him to get the ball over the linemen.

The scrambling style of play can sometimes drive defenses crazy. In Tarkenton's case, there were also times it drove Van Brocklin crazy. Van Brocklin once said kidding-

128

ly that the only time he ran was "out of sheer terror." But there was more than a grain of truth to the remark. He did feel that Francis scrambled more than he had to, that he was too inclined to forsake the game plan and ball-control strategy in favor of his specialty.

Friction developed between Van Brocklin and Tarkenton, not so much because of his scrambling, but because the club could never win consistently. Then late in the 1966 season the Vikings played the Falcons in Atlanta, where Fran makes his home. Van Brocklin kept Tarkenton on the bench throughout the entire game. He said he wanted to give some game experience to rookie quarterback Bob Terry. The young man was intercepted four times and the Vikings lost.

The incident burned Tarkenton and after the season was over he sent a letter of resignation to the Vikings. Soon after, he landed with the Giants. Tarkenton has all the natural gifts that a quarterback needs to be a scrambler. He's quick and resourceful and pressure doesn't bother him. He points out that the whole trend of pro football tactics has been toward flexibility and mobility (except in the case of Green Bay), and that all his twisting and dodging are simply part of that trend. He feels that in time it will be normal for every quarterback to roll out, to throw from the moving pocket, to work the bootleg and all the rest.

There's no doubt about it, the ability to scramble is a good one to have. It gets you yardage plenty of times in seemingly hopeless situations. But you can't build a team's offense around scrambling. Quite the contrary. The pocket passer, indeed, the whole concept of pocket protection is what serves as a basis for a team's offense. All your plays are mapped out with the pocket as the foundation. You work on pocket-based plays at training camp and in preparing for teams during the season. Your timing with your receivers is based upon the pocket idea. Of course, there are times you can scramble and be very successful at it. A scrambler can turn a game around or win one that seems lost. But in the long run, scrambling does more harm than good. You're going to sustain some big losses. You're going to get hit with some third-and-forty situations. You're going to lose to a weaker team once in a while.

There is no scramble play as such. Tarkenton never steps into the huddle and says, "O.K. This is a scramble. Everyone act accordingly." He calls conventional plays. But sometimes he'll call a play and then when he comes up to the ball, he'll see that the defenses are set to stop him. So while he's waiting for the snap, he'll decide he's going to scramble. He won't even stop at seven yards; he'll keep right on running. No pocket passer ever does this.

When the quarterback scrambles, everyone on the team has to scramble. The linemen have to run around with him in their attempt to defend. And the receivers, when they see the quarterback is out of the pocket, have to break from their patterns. Suppose the play calls for the receivers to break left, and they look back and see that the quarterback is scrambling right. They have to reverse direction and maneuver to get clear. In other words, there are no set plays; there's no scrambling offense as such. The receivers cut back and try to find a lane that's open. It's a melee. It's hard to put together a sustained drive when there's a lot of scrambling going on. Coaches are quick to point out that no team has ever won with a scrambler.

Under Tarkenton's exciting and creative direction, the Giants perked up. But Fran is no superman. The optimism of September was dimmed by the realities of November and December when the team lost more games than it won. They finished with a 7–7 record. The coaches wrote it off as a "building year." The following year would be a "performance year," they said. Of course, it wasn't.

CHAPTER SEVENTEEN

It was all Tarkenton in 1967. I was the forgotten man, the quarterback in limbo, playing only when a game was completely out of reach or safely in hand. I could never go through a season like that again.

I dreaded the thought of going to training camp. I knew what it was going to be like. When the day came to leave, I felt miserable. I was supposed to drive from our home in Bloomfield Hills, to Lima, Ohio, to pick up Joe Morrison, my roommate, and then we were going to go on to Fairfield together. But I spent the whole day fidgeting around the house, doing meaningless little things. I just couldn't bring myself to get into the car and start out. When I finally did leave, I was four or five hours behind schedule.

When the practice sessions started, I knew at once I was going to be traded. No one told me, but you catch on quick. We'd have a passing drill and I'd throw once or twice and then a coach would turn to one of the other quarterbacks and say, "All right, get in there," and that was my cue to get out of the way, to do something else.

Then Gary Wood was cut by the Saints and the Giants picked him up. Gary couldn't believe his good luck. The year before in New Orleans he had played a total of six and one-half minutes. In one game they had put him in as flanker. But Wood was a scrambler, and as such he fit into Sherman's scheme of things. The Giants still had Tom Kennedy, too. Four quarterbacks. No team can use *four* quarterbacks.

I didn't play a single minute in any of the pre-season games. I wasn't invited to attend quarterback meetings. Sherman didn't even want me working on the phones. He didn't want me making suggestions to Tarkenton or any of the other quarterbacks.

The last thing I wanted to do was let Sherman know how much he was hurting me. Whenever I did get a chance to run a scrimmage, I'd bark out the signals loud and clear, and I'd slap the ball really hard to the backs on the hand-offs, and I put more than the usual amount of snap in my passes. But it seemed the better I looked, the less Sherman used me.

To get in shape, I stayed late, after most of the guys had left the practice field, and worked with anyone who would stay with me. Usually I ended up passing to third- and fourth-string backs and receivers, fellows who were trying to make the team, some of them from the Westchester Bulls, a Giant farm team in the Continental League. I didn't care. I would have worked out with high school kids. I just wanted to get in shape.

Several times I talked to Allie.

"You're not using me; how do you expect me to get in shape?"

"We gotta see what the kid can do," was his standard answer. He meant Kennedy. "We gotta get him sharp for the season."

"I gotta get in shape, too."

"Well, we know what you can do. We're trying to find out what he can do."

And he'd always assure me that no trade was planned. But the newspapers were filled with rumors. Besides, I knew.

One hot, humid Saturday afternoon in August, we had

finished our morning workout, and four of us—Tucker, Bill Swain and Joe Morrison—were playing gin in the dorm. One of the kids who helped out the equipment manager came into the room and said that Sherman wanted to see me.

I knew this was it. When you're thirty-four and the coach sends for you, you feel it in the pit of your stomach. You know it's something big, but you don't know what. It's the uncertainty that gets you. Are you going to be traded, put on waivers, or just let go? You never know. When something is pending, a quarterback spends a lot of time running down the team rosters in his mind. "Is it going to be Green Bay? They've got Starr and Bratkowski. Washington? Jurgensen and Ninowski. Los Angeles? Gabriel and Plum. St. Louis? Well, the Cards have got some problems. Maybe it'll be the Cards." And so on.

Sherman had a cigarette going. He got to the point quickly. He had talked to Don Shula, head coach at Baltimore, and they had worked out a deal. I was going to the Colts.

"Well, I knew something was brewing," I said. "I knew I wasn't going to stay around here."

"No, no," Sherman protested. "This just came up. Shula called us."

"Well, I don't know what to do, Allie. I don't know if I should go. I want to talk it over with my wife before I give you a decision."

"Why don't you call Shula? Call him from here." Sherman indicated the phone, then left the room.

I knew Shula, of course. He had been the defensive coach in Detroit from 1960-1962, when I was there. When I got him on the phone, he explained the club wanted some experience behind Unitas.

"We're a little concerned about him," Shula said. "He's been having some problems with his arm."

"What about Jim Ward?" I asked. Ward was the No. 2 man with the Colts the year before. He was twenty-four. I didn't want to get slotted in back of him.

"Ward twisted his knee. He can't play."

Then Shula explained that the club had a good chance to win the championship and to get into the Super Bowl. "But we need a proven quarterback behind Johnny. We'd like to have you down here tomorrow."

"No," I said. "I don't know what I'm going to do. I want to talk it over with my wife."

"Well, there's not much time. There are only two exhibition games left and we want to get you as much work as possible."

"I just don't know, Don. I'll have to call you back."

I drove home. Jane and the kids had moved into an apartment in Darien, Connecticut, about a week before. Now they faced another move.

We weighed every alternative. If I refused to go to Baltimore, it would probably be the end. There was no place for me with the Giants. Sherman wanted me like he wanted leprosy. I was going to cost Shula merely a fourth round draft choice. If he had pressed Sherman, Don probably could have gotten me for six rolls of adhesive tape and a pair of second-hand shoulder pads. If I refused to go with the Colts, Sherman would undoubtedly send me somewhere else, to another and probably a much weaker team. I didn't want that. I remembered what it was like playing with the Giants in those first few games of 1966. I remembered all the body aches and blows to my psyche. I didn't want to be cannon fodder again. At best, it seemed, the future was sombre. When you're a quarterback and you're thirty-four, no coach is thinking of building around you. Everything is very short-term. But one thing was certain, I wasn't going to quit. I'd never give Sherman the satisfaction of saying, "Oh, Morrall? He quit on us."

Besides, I was really in top shape, in the best condition I had been in in years. I knew I could make a contribution. Maybe, with Johnny's arm and all, there would be a chance for me to play in Baltimore. And Shula was right—there was a very good possibility the team could go all the way.

I made up my mind. I called Shula.

"O.K.," I said. "I'll report. When do you want me?"

"Right away."

They always want you right away.

CHAPTER EIGHTEEN

I've often thought the wives of the players are the unsung heroes—or heroines—of professional football. They and the youngsters move about from city to city like displaced persons, yet you seldom hear any complaints.

You can't imagine how difficult it is for a player's wife to find housing that is attractive—even liveable—and reasonably priced. It's because of the short-term nature of her needs. She requires a house or apartment from about the time training begins to the end of the season, from about the middle of August to the end of December. Few landlords want to rent on that basis.

The problem is increased when there are children involved, and we have four—two boys, Matt, the oldest, Mitch, the youngest; and two girls, Mardi and Mindi. (My wife happens to like alliterative names.) In addition to the increased packing to be done (half the basement in our home in Bloomfield Hills is given over to the storage of wardrobe cases, standing ready for the next summer exodus), there is the school problem to face.

About a week or so before the deal was made for me to go to the Colts, Jane came East with the kids. That year we had worked out an exchange arrangement with Roger Shoals, a tackle with the Lions, whereby he moved into the home we owned in Bloomfield Hills, and we took over his apartment in Darien, Connecticut. But we only lived in it a week. The day Jane arrived was the same day that the Giants obtained Gary Wood from the Saints. I greeted her with this news at the airport. "Shall I bother to unpack?" she asked.

The next week the trade was made and I flew down to Baltimore to get ready for the season. Jane, after doling out the kids to neighbors and friends in Connecticut, came down the next weekend to launch a desperate search for housing. She got the newspapers and a radio station to make announcements about our plight but none of the calls she received panned out. One woman offered to rent us a house if we would look after her fourteen cats. A man called to say that he had a tenant house on a farm available if I would help out with the barnyard chores. And a couple of perverts called.

After a long search and some fervent pleading, Jane finally found a two-bedroom unfurnished apartment in suburban Towson. She rented some primitive furniture and bought kitchen utensils at Woolworth's. Dotty Shula and some of the other wives loaned us a vacuum cleaner and other appliances. In addition to the four youngsters, we have a live-in girl, and we're normally a five-bedroom family. When I came home to the apartment at night, it was seldom less than chaos. I was never able to start studying the Colt playbook until everyone was in bed and asleep, usually around eleven o'clock or so.

Jane feels that it's very important that the family move for the season to the city where I'm playing. I agree. Along about the middle of training season, after I've been away for two or three weeks, the youngsters begin to get a trifle hard to handle. They need a father's discipline. Moving's a chore, but we do it every year.

The first year we were in New York Jane almost rented a house that was located in a town called Turn of the

River, Connecticut, and plunk in the middle of a swamp. I wouldn't allow the family to move in. I imagined them all becoming drowning victims. But we were lucky to work out another exchange, this one with Darrell Dess, who was going to the Lions in the same deal that sent me to New York.

The next year we lived in a mansion, a magnificent twenty-nine room home on more than twenty acres of wooded hill-land near Stamford. It was paradise for the kids and within walking distance of a school. Don't ask me how Jane did it. She got it back the next season, too.

Before we moved into the home we now own in Bloomfield Hills, we owned only one other—in Pittsburgh, in suburban Bethel Park, actually. It was a split level. We moved into the house shortly before the team made a trip to the West Coast. While I was away Jane started the furnace for the first time and something went wrong and the house filled with thick black smoke. The builder replaced the furnace with a new one and it worked fine, but the house smelled like a fireman's glove.

That was only the beginning of our troubles. The house was perched on the side of a hill and had a steep sloping driveway. One day Jane came home from a shopping trip and was unloading packages from the car when it started rolling. It gathered speed, and Jane, eight months pregnant at the time, gave chase. The car barrelled into the street, lurched crazily through a neighbor's yard and finally flipped over. The damage was estimated at $1,400.

Then as a topper, a couple of days later I got the news I was being traded. I was not unhappy about leaving Pittsburgh. I figured no matter where I went things couldn't be much worse.

When you're the wife of a pro football player, Sunday has a special meaning. It's a day of apprehension and anxiety. If the team is out of town, the family watches the game on television. But Jane takes the kids to all the home games. And she sits tensely, never taking her eyes from the action. In Detroit, she used to worry that I wasn't going to play. Then when I did get in the game, she'd worry that I might get injured or that I'd be made to look bad. Sometimes I think she has a much more difficult time in the stands than I do on the field. The Super Bowl was torture for her. It was a trial for the kids, too. Mardi, ten at the time, sobbed uncontrollably. Matt, eleven, became stone silent.

One of the most hectic periods we ever endured took place right after we won the NFL championship in 1968. The game was played on December 29 and the lease on our apartment expired on January 1. Almost as soon as the game was over, we had to go through the frenzy of packing and getting our belongings back to Bloomfield Hills. We loaded everything into one of those you-rent-it trailers, but just before we set out, Jane rebelled. "I can't spend all that time in the back seat with all those kids," she wailed, "I just can't." Three of the youngsters had virus infections and were shooting high temperatures. So I took her and the kids to the airport and put them on a plane, then I headed back alone.

Jane made a spectacular arrival. When the plane landed in Detroit, Mitch, then barely a year old, who was seated on his mother's lap, jounced forward and struck his face on the seat in front, tearing a small gash in his chin. It wasn't serious but he spurted blood all over the place. All the other kids just screamed. Jane, bless her, loaded the youngsters into a friend's car and drove straight for the

140

family pediatrician. It was late at night when she arrived at his home, and he came to the door sleepy-eyed.

"We're back! We're back!" she exclaimed.

I'm not too sure he was happy about it.

CHAPTER NINETEEN

One day not long after I had joined the Colts the team was scheduled to play San Francisco, and the day before the game we had a light workout at Memorial Stadium. After we were finished and were coming off the field, the Forty-Niners were coming on, and I saw Y. A., and I stopped to talk to him.

"I don't know what's going to happen tomorrow," I said. "This system is really complicated. And it's even to the right and odd to the left; that's got me more confused."

"Don't worry," Y. A. said, and he was laughing. "Just throw a pass and then give them a draw. That's all there is to it."

Y. A.'s breezy attitude was no help. I had some doleful moments calling signals for the Colts—at least at first.

Learning pro formations and a team's system of signal calling is something like learning a foreign language, say French. One day you reach a stage where you're able to think in French. It's the same with calling signals. Before a play, an experienced quarterback knows exactly how he wants to set his team. He visualizes the formation in his mind. Then it's merely a matter of calling out the right terms, of expressing verbally how he wants the players set. But it takes time to gain this facility.

Besides the formation, the quarterback must designate the play he wants to run, the number on which the ball is to be snapped, and he may also give special blocking assignments. Each team—naturally—has its own system. It is a matter of fact that formations and plays do not change a great deal from team to team. What does change is the nomenclature. Some teams use colors to designate types of plays. Others use numbers. On one team, quick-opening plays may be known as the "quick" series; on another, they're called the "pop" series. In other words, it's more a matter of learning a new vocabulary than learning a whole new system. Once Johnny Unitas said that we should get the Players' Association to insist that coaches standardize football terminology. He said it kiddingly, of course. There's no chance this will ever happen. Each coach has his own terminology and expects the players to adapt.

Take hole numbering. Most teams in the National League number the holes with the even numbers to the left and the odd numbers to the right. Like this:

(E)   (T)   (G)   (⊗)   (G)   (T)   (E)
 6   4   2   0   1   3   5   7

This system was introduced by the Chicago Bears in the late 1930's. All teams use it or a variation of it.

Each of the backfield positions is also numbered—like this:

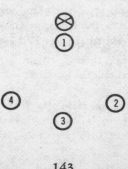

In recent years, it's become normal for the No. 2 back-field man to line-up as a flanker, with the fullback, the No. 3 back, running from a halfback position. It looks like this:

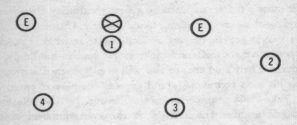

A quarterback uses these numbers when he calls a play in the huddle, and each player knows exactly who is going to carry the ball and where he is going. For instance, when I was with Detroit, and I wanted to send left halfback Hop Cassady off right tackle, I'd say, "forty-three"—the No. 4 back into the No. 3 hole. It's as simple as that.

But, as I said, the system is subject to variations. After I was traded to the Giants, I found that they had the same hole numbering system as the Lions, so I had relatively few problems. Then, after ten years' experience with the system, I was sent to the Colts, and at Baltimore it was just the opposite, odd to the left and even to the right—like this:

And the backfield positions were numbered in the opposite way:

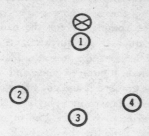

As you can imagine, I put the wrong number on things a few times. I'd be thinking one play, one picture, and the other players would be thinking something else. It took a good many weeks for me to get really comfortable with the Baltimore system. Look at it this way. Suppose I tell you that you're to think of your right arm as your left, and your left arm as your right. And to think of your right leg as your left, and your left leg as your right. Then I tell you to touch your right leg, or raise your left arm. You can do it, but you have to think a second or two before you move. In play-calling, that second can be disastrous. I had to eat the ball a few times because I'd be turning the wrong way—that is, the backs would be going in the opposite direction, away from the handoff.

Once in a game against the Los Angeles Rams, Shula sent in a play we called "thirty-four slant." In both New York and Detroit we had a thirty-four slant, too. The Giants used it a great deal in short yardage situations. It meant that I was to handoff to the fullback who was to hit the hole off left tackle. But with the Colts, thirty-four slant meant that the halfback was to carry and hit the hole off right tackle. Well, when the play came in from Shula, my immediate reaction was to hand to the fullback, the New York version. And that's what I did. Everyone else was thinking the Baltimore system, of course. Tom Matte, instead of coming by for the handoff, was going the other way, much to my surprise and chagrin. I knew instantly that I had made a mistake. Matte did, too, but we both recovered. I pumped once and then tossed him a soft lateral. He grabbed it and got a first down.

Another time Shula sent in a play we called "ride thirty-five," a belly series play where I'm supposed to fake to the fullback and hand to the halfback. Well, when the play came in, I took it to be a give to the fullback. In New York or Detroit, that's what I was supposed to do on any "thirty-five" play. We ran it off and Jerry Hill came by leading Matte, intent upon blocking out the middle linebacker. I slapped the ball into Hill's stomach, and when I didn't take it away, he got this stunned look. It was like I had slipped him a hot poker. But he instinctively grabbed hold of the ball and kept on going. Then Matte came by and when he saw what had happened he yelled, "*I* get the ball! *I* get the ball!" I turned in time to see Hill spin off the linebacker and struggle for a first down. It was a hairy moment.

The way the Colts numbered assignments and plays was only part of the problem. Their overall offensive system was more complicated than any I had ever encountered before. They had more plays and more formations. And certain plays were meant to be used only against specific defenses so you had to be extremely careful to read the opposition defense, read it accurately, and put in the right play. This was a new twist for me. In the past, teams that I had been with allowed me, as quarterback, to make my own judgment as to what play to call against a particular defense. Not at Baltimore; it was all spelled out for you.

If the strong side linebacker and the middle linebacker were blitzing, you were supposed to shoot the ball to Mackey, just drop it to him. Of if you called a pass pattern with Jimmy Orr as the primary receiver, and you went up to the line of scrimmage and saw that the weak side safety was prepared to pick him up, you forgot about Jimmy. Instead, Willie Richardson became your primary receiver.

Y. A. Tittle, after he was traded to the Giants from the Forty-Niners, two teams with numbering systems that were opposite, experienced similar problems. He'd go up to the line of scrimmage and look over the defense, and if he spotted a weakness, then he'd check-off, put a new play in. But in his first games with the Giants he'd forget how his fullback was set, to the right or left. If he was set left, and Y. A. called a thirty-four slant—sending the fullback off left tackle—everything was fine. But if he called a thirty-five slant, disaster would result. So in check-off situations, Y. A. got into the habit of looking back to see how his fullback was lined up. This was his tipoff. I learned to do the same thing in Baltimore.

So I not only had to learn new plays, new formations and new terminology, I had to concentrate more on reading defenses and reacting with the correct play. Compared to Baltimore, the Giants' system was child's play.

This careful attention to detail typified much of the Colts' operation. End coach Dick Bielski watched the receivers to see to it that their moves didn't become stereotyped. If a man was supposed to break outside, and he had gotten into the habit of veering inside just before he went out, Bielski would get him to vary his route. Things like that.

The Colts system called for the receivers to run their patterns in a very meticulous fashion. On most pass patterns, you have a primary receiver, a secondary receiver and a third man. You look first for the primary man. If he's covered or has been taken out of the play, you go to the second man and, last, the third man. Well, at Baltimore the patterns run by each of the receivers were staggered so that the men came open in sequence, one after another, with the primary receiver first. At other teams, when I'd be forced to go to my No. 2 man, I'd see that he had already completed his break, and that the defensive man had recovered. The same with the No. 3 man. But this seldom happened with the Colt receivers.

The game plans were another example of Colt thoroughness. A basic offensive game plan is prepared on mimeographed sheets and handed out to each player. It features a running and passing "ready list," a dozen or so plays of each type which the coaches feel will work with success. The plan also evaluates the opposition players. It says things like: "#23 can be beaten when isolated in overs, hooks, and turns," or "#83 is very inside conscious. I believe you can run outside him."

The game plan also gives "frequencies"; every phase of the opposing team's offense and defense is expressed in percentages. How often does the team blitz on a first-down-and-ten situation, when it is second down and long yardage, etc.? How often does the team pass, run, stunt, use a zone, etc.? On the Colts, these frequences were far more comprehensive than any I had ever seen. Some teams based their game plans on a scout's report and three or four game films, but the Colts used films from six or seven previous games. So we had a great mass of new information to digest before each game.

Don McCafferty, the Colts' backfield coach, was my chief tutor. He was a careful, thorough, and—thankfully —a patient man.

CHAPTER TWENTY

Carroll D. Rosenbloom, the owner of the Colts, is not a man who likes to finish second. One day he addressed the team before we went out on the field for a practice session. Our first game of the season was about a week away. All the coaches, all the players were there.

It was just a short talk, but it left no doubt in anyone's mind about his intense desire to win. Coming close would not be enough, he said. He explained how in the past he had shifted personnel and changed coaches, even coaches who had been successful (he had dropped Weeb Ewbank after the 1962 season, just three years after Weeb had won the NFL title) in his efforts to win the championship, and he said he'd do it again. This kind of jolted some players. Shula was among those present and he owned an outstanding record, one that had earned him praise from every quarter. But Rosenbloom made it clear that even Shula's job wasn't to be considered secure—unless we won.

The evidence indicates that Baltimore's personnel had changed considerably from year to year, yet the club seems always to be stocked with skilled players at every position. When a front line player retires, a talented newcomer moves right in.

In 1964, the year the Colts won the Western Division title, but lost to the Browns in the championship playoff, the team lined up like this in offense:

SE—Ray Berry   TE—John Mackey
LT—Bob Vogel   QB—John Unitas

LG—Jim Parker	RB—Tom Matte
C —Dick Szymanski	RB—J. W. Lockett
RG—Alex Sandusky	FL—Jimmy Orr
RT—George Preas	

For the Super Bowl, just five years later, we had this offensive lineup:

SE—Jimmy Orr	TE—John Mackey
LT—Bob Vogel	QB—Earl Morrall
LG—Glenn Ressler	FL—Willie Richardson
C —Bill Curry	RB—Tom Matte
RG—Dan Sullivan	RB—Jerry Hill
RT—Sam Ball	

Bob Vogel was the only holdover in the interior line. And Mackey and Orr were the only first string veterans among the receivers.

The defensive team looked like this in 1964:

LE —Gino Marchetti	RLB—Don Shinnick
LT —Jim Colvin	LC —Jim Welch
RT —Fred Miller	RC —Lenny Lyles
RE —Ordell Braase	LS —Andy Nelson
LLB—W. J. Burkett	RS —Wendell Harris
MLB—Bill Pellington	

And for the Super Bowl, the defensive line-up was:

LE —Bubba Smith	LS —Jerry Logan
LT —Billy Ray Smith	RS —Rick Volk
RT —Fred Miller	LLB—Mike Curtis
RE —Ordell Braase	MLB—Dennis Gaubatz
LC —Bobby Boyd	RLB—Don Shinnick
RC —Lenny Lyles	

151

It's easy to see that wholesale changes were made. Interestingly, of all the new regulars, all but Gaubatz, Curry, Billy Ray Smith and myself were products of the player draft, a tribute to the ability of Shula and Upton Bell, the son of Bert Bell, and the chief talent scout for the club.

End Ray Berry, tackle Jim Parker, and halfback Lenny Moore, three standout veterans, left the Colts the year I joined the team. But replacements were ready. Willie Richardson had assumed a starting role as a wide receiver. Sam Ball took over at tackle. And the club traded to get Timmy Brown, one of the game's finer running backs, from the Eagles.

The job at Detroit was Shula's first coaching post. As a defensive back, he spent two seasons with the Browns, four with the Colts, and one with Washington. He played offense in college, at John Carroll University in Cleveland.

He did an outstanding job in Detroit. He was zealous and well-liked and more than equal to the task of coaching the Lions' outstanding players, Schmidt, Karras, and the others. He installed many varied and sophisticated defensive alignments. As I stated earlier, Detroit's defense in those days was the best in the league.

Shula became head coach of the Colts in 1963, steered the club to the Western Conference championship in 1964, and managed to get the Colts a tie for the title again in 1965 despite the late-season loss of both Unitas and Gary Cuozzo, then the No. 2 quarterback. But Green Bay beat the Colts in sudden-death overtime.

Baltimore finished second in the Western Conference in 1966. The next year the Colts won eleven games, lost one, and tied two, but they didn't even win the Coastal Division (the Western Conference had been split into two four-team divisions, the Coastal Division and the Central Division). The Rams had exactly the same record as the Colts but they were awarded the championship because they had outscored the Colts in their two meetings.

I found Shula to be eminently fair. He never prejudged a player; he made decisions on the basis of merit, always with the good of the team uppermost in his mind. I felt he was a master of getting the most out of his coaches, at coordinating their skills and knowledge—and that, after all, is a head coach's foremost responsibility. All head coaches are surrounded by experienced assistants, five or six of them. The best head coaches give each assistant meaningful duties and responsibilities, yet supervise and coordinate with such efficiency that a certain oneness comes out of all the activity. At Baltimore there was no inter-team competition between players or between the offensive and defensive teams as there was in Detroit. We were one—a solid unit.

I think it's an often overlooked fact, but Shula has been one of the most successful coaches in NFL history. After the 1968 season, his sixth at Baltimore, he had a composite record of 65-18-13. Vince Lombardi compiled a 89-29-3 record in nine seasons at Green Bay. Lombardi won 72 per cent of the time, Shula 76 per cent.

I was a bit awed by the Colts. They were skilled, poised and seasoned, and they had more determination than any team I had ever been with, much more. At the first practice, I could feel this tremendous desire, an urge not only to win, but to win it all. They believed in themselves. They weren't going to be denied.

Tom Matte, the Colts leading rusher, was solid and dependable, just the kind of a guy you need when you're down near the goal line. He could also pass on the option play, and catch passes. He caught twenty-five during the 1968 season, a terrific showing. When a back rips out of the backfield for a pass, a linebacker always picks him up, but despite this Matte had the knack of getting to the open spot. I completed a number of passes to Matte that I know couldn't have been caught by any other back in the league.

Matte was not the fastest back in the world or the flashiest, and year in and year out the Colts tried to come up with a runner to replace him. But when the season opened Tom would be in his familiar spot in the starting lineup.

He was a heady runner. He knew how to read blocks, how to find and hit that crack of daylight. The tension of playing was always tough for him to take, however. He'd do anything he could to take his mind off an upcoming game. Of course, the annual competition for his job didn't do his nervous system any good.

Before the 1968 season began, the Colts acquired Timmy Brown from the Philadelphia Eagles. Brown is a topflight performer, exceptionally fast, a gamebreaker, and he figured to give Tom a close battle. Early in the season, Matte, long bothered by ulcers, went to his doctor for a checkup. The next day when he came into the locker room, someone shouted out, "How'd you make out, Tom? Did you pass your physical?"

"They found another ulcer," Matte said, "a third one."

Alex Hawkins was listening. From the other side of the room, he yelled over to Tom. "What did you name it, Matte? Timmy Brown?"

Even Matte laughed.

During the 1965 season, Matte became an instant celebrity. Not long before the final game with the Rams, Unitas injured a knee, and Gary Cuozzo, the back-up quarterback, suffered a shoulder separation. Shula moved Matte into the quarterbacking job. His previous experience dated to his sophomore season at Ohio State, seven years before.

He didn't have much time to prepare for the Los Angeles game because he came down with the flu and missed some practices. Everything was jammed into two or three days. In the locker room before the game, they wound a strip of adhesive tape around his wrist and printed the key plays and formations on it, a unique crib sheet.

At one stage during the game, the Rams backed up the Colts to the 1 yard line. In the huddle Matte called a running play that he hoped would spring loose Lenny Moore. Just as the team lined up, Dan Sullivan turned around from his slot at left guard.

"Tom," he said, "you'd better change the play. You've got Lenny Moore running into a goal post."

Tom changed it.

Tom was less than artful in the way he ran with the ball. Alex Karras labeled him a garbage can halfback during a game in Detroit in 1967. The Lions were getting beat, and badly. Karras was in a foul mood. Late in the game Matte bulled his way off tackle, by Karras, and into the end zone. Karras fumed. He turned to Matte and said, "It's bad enough getting beat by you guys, but what I can't stomach is getting scored on by a garbage can halfback like you."

Jim Parker, then a guard for the Colts, and a onetime teammate of Matte's at Ohio State, almost died laughing, and he ran off the field shouting to the other guys, "We've got a garbage can halfback." At an awards banquet later in the year Shula presented Matte with a replica of a garbage can bearing an engraved brass plate, thus giving official status to the nickname.

Fullback Jerry Hill I rated the toughest man in the league, bar none. He was sturdy—five-foot-eleven, 220—and strong. As a runner, he was no trickster, no fancy Dan, but he'd put his head down and batter his way forward like a Sherman tank. He was a real hard-nosed guy on a run.

Hill was also a vicious blocker. He'd hit with every ounce of strength he owned on play after play. When Jerry formed part of my pocket protection and a linebacker would red dog, Jerry would step right up and stick him. It was like having a man with a gun there. The next time the guy came in he'd kind of feel his way. "Where's Hill?" he'd be thinking.

We played Los Angeles early in the season and on one play I went back to throw. Maxie Baughan, the Rams' 230-pound linebacker, was blitzing. Jerry went for him. Maxie saw Jerry coming and he put out his hands to turn him aside, but Jerry slipped underneath, hurling his body sideways across Maxie's knees. You could see the pain distort Maxie's face as his knees bent back and he collapsed and just lay there. They helped him off the field and I knew he was through for the day, probably for the season. He did come back the next week, however. I give him a lot of credit.

Hill himself has no conception of what pain is. He plays with small hurts and with big ones, too.

Hill, however, suffered a serious knee injury and missed the last four games of the regular season, but Terry Cole, a rookie from Indiana, filled in and did a remarkable job. He accelerates quickly and he's real fast. Enemy linebackers underrated him. On sweep plays, they'd often take the wrong angle on Cole, figuring they'd meet him at the sidelines, but Terry would make the turn and be racing down the sideline before the defense could catch him.

When Terry cracked some ribs in the last game of the season, Preston Pearson took over at fullback. Pearson went to Illinois but he never played college football; basketball was his game, and you could tell this from his quick starts and stops and his all around elusiveness. He caught two critical passes in our second game with the Rams and turned both receptions into touchdowns.

The new players, such as Cole and Pearson, really benefited from the Colts' winning spirit. I've been on teams where the rookies are troubled and apprehensive. They're always asking themselves, "Have I gotten this assignment right?" or "Am I making the right move?" They begin to doubt their skills. But this didn't happen on the Colts. They got caught up in the spirit of confidence that prevailed and just went out and did the right thing.

Flanker Willie Richardson had the speed of a sprinter and skillful hands, and was adept at using his body to shield off defensemen, enabling him to wrap up the ball. He could really leap, so if you put the ball high above Willie and his defender, Willie would be the one who'd get it. He didn't have the moves of, say, Jimmy Orr, but he had more speed. He was very strong and was never afraid to fight for the ball. In the latter part of the season, he made some fantastic catches for us in key games.

A quarterback couldn't have a better receiver than John Mackey. He has to be rated as pro football's best tight end. Most strong side ends have a speciality; they're superior as blockers, or runners, or their genius is short passes or long ones. But Mackey, with his speed and awesome power, was skilled in all of these. Plus he was shrewd. He could read defenses so that he knew where the hole was going to be and he knew the moves he had to make to

157

get there. He was a big problem for the strong side safety; he couldn't play him close because of Mackey's speed. Mackey would run right by him. Yet the safety couldn't play off Mackey either, because once he made the catch and got rolling, he'd run right over most defenders.

During the 1968 season, we started using Mackey on end-around plays, and he liked to run these. Once during a scrimmage, Mackey came back to the huddle and called out, "Earl," and I looked up to see him take his finger and trace a small semicircle in the center of his chest. I didn't understand. He did it again. "It's the end-around, Earl," he said. "Call the end-around." He gave me this signal often during the season, and I'd slot the play whenever I could.

Some receivers have a sixth sense, a special "feel," that helps them to spot gaps in the defense. They have a thorough understanding of the play that's been called and, of course, they know the pattern they're supposed to run, and when they put this information together, it enables them to get to the right spot at precisely the right time. They're uncanny at it. Jimmy Orr has this ability. He could do it when we were both with the Steelers in 1958, but today the skill is more highly developed. Terry Barr and Hop Cassady with the Lions, Joe Morrison of the Giants, and Max McGee of the Packers were other receivers who were similarly skilled. There are many others. They may not have blinding speed, but they just have this special knowledge of where the hole is going to open up and how to get there.

With a receiver like Orr, a quarterback has the maximum opportunity to connect. You can throw before he hits the hole, or lead him into the center of the hole, or even be a little bit late and still complete the pass, whereas some receivers are through the hole or by it in the blink of an eye.

Jimmy also knew exactly how he was being played. You could say to Jimmy, "What can you beat him on?" and he'd answer, "Give me an outside pattern," and you could be sure the information was reliable. And a series or two later you could say to him, "Can you beat him outside again?" and he might answer, "No, the guy's moved outside; bring it down and in." And he'd be right again.

Tom Mitchell was another fine receiver. A tight end, he played behind Mackey. He had superb moves and when he got the ball he was tough to bring down. The first four times he caught passes in 1968, he scored a touchdown. Shula used him in a variety of ways, as a receiver or blocker when we needed short yardage, and on the special punting and kickoff teams. He was only twenty-three. He's got a lot of good years ahead of him.

Mitchell was also a fine blocker. So was Ray Perkins, who played behind Jimmy Orr. He was a battler, always ready to fight for the ball. Gail Cogdill, a flanker whom I knew from Detroit, joined the Colts late in the season. He got into three games. Cogdill had good size—he was six-foot-two and weighed 200—and good speed. In Detroit, he wanted the football on every play. He did in Baltimore, too.

Alex Hawkins, a reserve end, a veteran, was the team comedian, the needler. He kidded players and coaches alike. He often was assigned to special teams and he played in a reckless fashion. During training camp in 1968, the coaches timed each player's speed over various measured distances. Alex was timed at 4.9 seconds for the forty-yard dash, a deplorable showing. Shula ribbed him. "My God, Alex," he said, "we thought you were fast, but it looks like we're going to have to put you in with the linemen. Why I don't know if you'll even be able to make the kickoff team."

"Don't worry about it, coach," Alex replied. "You watch. On those kickoffs I'll beat all those 4.4 guys."

And he did. The fast guys would be cautious, looking for the blockers. Not Alex. He flew down there.

Bob Vogel, the left tackle, while not overly big for his position—six-foot-five, 245—was a shrewd tactician. He'd let an opponent make his move, then counter. Sometimes he'd turn his man and sometimes he simply cut him down but he always kept him guessing. He played the last three games of the season with a broken bone in his forearm and often felt excruciating pain.

Glenn Ressler, at left guard, was the team's quiet man. You'd get a "yes" or "no" from him once in a while, but not much else. He was the power man on the pull. Anytime you watched a game film, you couldn't help but notice that Ressler delivered on every single play.

Dick Szymanski, a thirteen-year veteran, and Bill Curry, who had been obtained from the Packers, alternated at center in the early stages of the season. Then Szymanski injured his ankle and Curry took over fulltime. Solid and dependable, Curry proved a real "find."

Dan Sullivan, a right guard, had some contract problems with the front office early in the year, but the dispute never affected his play. He was steady and strong whether blocking or pulling.

Sam Ball, the right tackle, a three-year man, had taken over the previous season for Jim Parker. He was an aggressive player, always full of fire.

Taken on the basis of sheer skill, the individuals that comprised the Colts' defensive unit were not the best I had ever seen. There were players on the Lions team in the early 1960's who were bigger, faster, and more agile. But taken together, the Colts were the best by far. They meshed together beautifully.

They used a standard zone. The weak side cornerback and the two safetymen rotated toward the strong side and covered the three deep zones, while the strong side cornerback and the linebackers covered the short zones. This system seemed to bring out the best in each man. Take Bobby Boyd, our left cornerback. Forget the fact he was bald. Forget that he was only five-foot-eleven and weighed 192, and that he wasn't the fastest back in the league. But Boyd was as knowledgeable about the game as any man you'll ever find, and he had craftiness to go with his knowledge. He made a detailed study of each man he had to cover and he always seemed to know precisely where he was going, and when he moved, he always took the shortest route. He never made his move too early. He'd lay off until the quarterback was ready to throw. He did this in practice a lot, and you'd think you had him beat or out of position and you'd throw, and suddenly Boyd would be there and he'd pick it off or knock it down. The zone defense allowed Boyd to play in this fashion. If we had used a man to man defense, he'd have had to cover one guy all over the field. A really fast receiver would beat him. But in the zone he could lay off a man, disguising what he planned to do until the last second.

Some teams never blitz. One problem with the blitz is that if you don't get a man through, the offense has it made. The passer can take his time and each receiver has only one man to beat. But Baltimore seldom got burned blitzing, even when we failed to shoot a guy through.

Boyd and Lenny Lyles, the other cornerbacks, have to get credit for this. Very seldom were they beat deep.

Our defensive team was constantly adjusting to meet the situation. The linebackers were experts in stunting, moving in and out before the snap. In fact, they had a whole array of gyration, a feature that Baltimore teams of the future are likely to emphasize. Suppose our team was prepared to blitz and the opposing quarterback, sensing this, checked off to go into a formation he believed would be more appropriate.

The Baltimore linebacking corps—Mike Curtis on the left, Dennis Gaubatz in the middle, and Don Shinnick— were the best in the business. Take Curtis; he was All Pro in 1968, a selection that surprised no one. He had fantastic speed and the reactions of a jungle cat. And he had a superb mean streak. He loved to hit. He wasn't satisfied with simply bringing a man down; he always tried to smash him into the ground or bowl him over backwards. He was always fierce—a key man.

Rich Volk, who had become a starter during 1967, his rookie year, was a natural as a free safety. He had great range and no one could read keys faster. Jerry Logan, on the other side, was always steady and reliable. Bubba Smith, the man built like a mountain, was the defensive end on the left side, paired with Ordell Braase, a twelve-year veteran, and a strong and steady pass rusher. Bubba was six-foot-seven, 295; Braase was six-foot-four, 245, giving the Colts a pair of defensive ends bigger than their defensive tackles.

Bubba had played the tackle's spot in 1967, his rookie season, but was moved to end the next year, a switch that made him a better player. He played next to Billy Ray Smith, from Arkansas, a ten-year man. The two liked to kid one another. One day Bubba stormed into the locker room and over to where Billy Ray was seated. He looked down and said, "Billy Ray, what's this I hear? Someone told me that you're in favor of segregation."

"Whoever told you that is a damn liar," said Billy Ray, and he jumped to his feet. "I don't want segregation. What I'm in favor of is slavery." Bubba was stunned—until they both started laughing.

Sometimes Bubba is compared to Big Daddy Lipscomb, the tackle who played for the Colts in the late 1950's and who has become something of a legend. But Bubba is bigger and faster, plus they differ in technique. On a pass rush, Big Daddy would pluck away your blockers one by one until you stood there naked and alone. Bubba was less deliberate. I remember in a game against Atlanta, Bill Harris of the Falcons tried to turn Bubba's end. Leading the blocking was Dan Grimm, a 245-pound guard, a six-year veteran in the league. Well, Bubba was waiting and when Grimm made his move, Bubba seized him, hoisted him into the air and then flung him at the ball-carrier, bowling him over for a three-yard loss.

But the big thing about the Colts was their desire, their tremendous will to win. Other teams that I had been with would hold meetings during the season in an attempt to build enthusiasm or to give the team a lift. The coaches would leave and then individual players would get up and each would tell why he felt the upcoming game was so important, and why we should all put out. But the Colts only did this once or twice and in each case the meeting was surprisingly brief. The players seemed to agree with Unitas who, at one of the meetings, remarked, "Meetings don't do much for you. You can talk all you want but actions speak louder than words." The Colts had spirit, but they didn't have to work to generate it; it was innate.

When the team left the locker room for a game, they were soaring. I remember seeing game films and watching Tom Mitchell and Roy Hilton, who played the opposite ends when the Colts kicked off. They'd target on the ball carrier and head for him like bullets from a rifle barrel. When they hit, they tackled with a terrible ferocity. It was like someone had uncaged them. This kind of thing is contagious. A player would see Mitchell and he'd make up his mind to equal or surpass him in aggressiveness.

I remember attending a luncheon with some of the guys a few days after I had been with the club. Each of us was asked to come to the microphone and say a few words about the upcoming season. When it came Sam Ball's turn, he got up and explained how the club had been so close in the past and how they were determined not to let the title slip away again.

Said Sam: "In my part of the country (he was from Kentucky), we've got an expression that covers this situation: 'Let the big dog eat.'"

Well, when Sam drawled it out, the audience roared. But Sam didn't crack a smile. He was grimly serious. The whole team was. The big dog was mighty hungry.

CHAPTER TWENTY-ONE

John F. Steadman, sports editor of the Baltimore *News American*, once wrote that the only thing Johnny Unitas hasn't accomplished for the Baltimore Colts is walking across the waves of Chesapeake Bay. "Of course," said Steadman, "he's never tried."

I knew well what Johnny Unitas could do. I had been watching him perform for twelve years.

While our careers had begun about the same time, they had often taken opposite turns. I was an All American at Michigan State. Unitas went to Louisville and never won any All American honors; in fact, his entire college career went virtually unnoticed. In 1956, the year I quarter-backed Michigan State in the Rose Bowl Game, Johnny was playing semi-pro football for the Bloomfield Rams, Bloomfield being a suburb of Pittsburgh. I was the No. 1 draft choice of the Forty-Niners and received a salary that was somewhat commensurate with that status, while Unitas, a free agent, was signed by Don Kellett, then the Colts' General Manager, for the cost of an eighty-five cent telephone call. The contract, Kellett told Unitas, would be for $7,000. Johnny quickly signed.

It was all different, of course, in the pros. While I was being shuttled from one team to another and in and out of the starting line-up, Johnny was making football history in Baltimore. I'm not going to recount all of his achievements here, but in the National Football League Record Manual, Unitas' records take up virtually a whole page. After Johnny joined the team, the Colts never once had a losing season. The glory years were 1958 and 1959, when Baltimore won the NFL title.

Unitas throws the ball in classic pro style—straight overhand. But just before he releases, he rolls his hand inward slightly. It travels at bullet-speed, but receivers say it's easier to handle. Johnny's ability to set up fast is one of his greatest assets. He gets back there lightning fast, faster than anyone I know. And he gets rid of the ball quickly.

From working with Unitas, I came to realize another of his gifts: he can read defenses the way most people read a calendar. I don't believe I know another quarterback who comes close to him in this skill. He really knows his keys. With just a quick glance, he can tell where to go with the ball. It's really uncanny. I remember a pass he completed to John Mackey in one of the exhibition games. Three defensive men were keyed on Mackey. Unitas went back only three steps, then fired. If he had delayed the pass as much as half a second more, if he had thrown it any earlier, it would have been knocked down or intercepted. But it was perfect.

Unitas can scramble. He can run. He calls a heady game. And he has this great confidence, the confidence—maybe it's courage—to do the thing he really wants to do. He is probably the most dangerous quarterback the game has ever known.

In 1967, Johnny had as good a year as any quarterback can hope to have. His throwing elbow gave him some pain —it had been bothering him off and on for three or four years—but it didn't hamper his effectiveness one iota. The Colts piled up win after win and when the season came down to the final game, they were still undefeated. They had been tied twice. To win the Coastal Division title, they had to beat the Rams in the final game of the season. Well, they didn't. They came up flat, and Johnny spent most of the day picking himself up off the turf at Memorial Coliseum. The Rams' front four got to him seven times. One of the best seasons in Baltimore's history had gone for nothing.

It was one of Johnny's best years, too. He threw more passes than he ever had before in a single season—a total of 436, or an average of about thirty-one a game. They gained 3428 yards, the second highest total of his career, and accounted for twenty touchdowns—certainly not statistics that a sore-armed quarterback might accrue. He was voted the league's Most Valuable Player for the second time in his career.

When I joined the Colts at their training camp in Westminster, Maryland, there were two other quarterbacks in camp—Terry Southall and Jimmy Ward. Southall was cut from the squad soon after I arrived. Ward was recovering from cartilage damage to his right knee. In a pre-season game several weeks before, he had called a quarterbackkeep to the outside. He faked the handoff, then cut right, picking up a perfect block from Jerry Hill that sprung him loose. The track ahead was clear. Then suddenly Ward's right knee gave way and he went down like someone had poleaxed him. No one was near him; he just collapsed. Fortunately, the damage to his knee wasn't serious enough to warrant surgery.

Ward is likely to be Baltimore's quarterback of the future. He's intelligent. He has a strong arm. He works hard. All he needs is game experience and Shula is sure to see that he gets it.

There were two exhibition games left on the schedule. The first took us to Miami to play the Dolphins. Johnny started and played the entire first half. I played most of the second half.

After the game, Johnny's arm swelled up. No one got excited, least of all Johnny. It was tendonitis, a condition that had plagued Johnny for several years. The tendons, as it was explained to me, are bundles of tiny white fibers, like straps, that bind down and connect the muscles to the bones. Under the strain of throwing, the tendons in Johnny's arm in the area of the elbow became painfully swollen and inflamed. Sometimes the malady is called "tennis elbow." Unitas never complained, although I know it hurt. He disdained the use of drugs like cortisone or Novocaine. To a professional, pain is part of the game, and Unitas is 110 per cent professional. He just accepted it.

The next week we went to Dallas to play the Cowboys, the last of our pre-season games. Shula explained that he intended to start Johnny, then use me in the second quarter, and then have Johnny take over again after the half. And if the game went well, I'd go back in, perhaps in the fourth quarter.

It was a night game and played in the Cotton Bowl. It attracted a near capacity crowd of 69,520. It was warm, but a sharp breeze made it pleasant.

Johnny started and was as slick as ever. Early in the first period, he hit Mackey with a pass, and the play covered 84 yards and got us a touchdown. Following Shula's plan, I played the second period.

Dallas kicked off to begin the third quarter. On first down, Johnny went back to pass. Mackey was his target. His arm may have been cold; remember, he had sat out the second quarter and then sat out the half. It wasn't a long pass, but he snapped it off, turning his hand

168

abruptly to the left as he released. Something "popped." Watching him out there, you knew something had gone wrong. You could see it on his face; the narrow eyes, the tight lips. But Johnny stayed in; he wouldn't quit. But whenever he threw, the ball kind of floated. It had no zip. And he couldn't put it where he wanted to.

He kept driving himself, continuing to throw and to move the team. I don't know how he did it; I don't know where he got the guts. Anxiety was building on the sidelines. "Get him outta there," I heard Bobby Boyd tell the team doctor. "Tell him he's gonna ruin his arm."

Johnny played through the third quarter and into the fourth. The score was 10–10. Dallas punted, but it was weak. We took over on their 40. Johnny completed two short passes, working the ball to the Cowboy 14. Two running plays were stopped and then a holding penalty made it third and twenty-five. A long pass was the obvious play. Johnny took the snap and pedaled back, his arm cocked. He threw. The ball traveled slow and along a humpbacked course and it plopped to the ground way short of the target. Every pair of eyes turned to look at Johnny. Grim, his head down, he was walking toward the sidelines and his left hand gripped his right elbow. Shula sent me in to finish up.

I don't think anyone realized how serious the injury was at the time. They thought it was the tendonitis. But in the days that followed, it became obvious it was something more. Johnny's arm puffed up and turned black and blue in the area below the elbow. It hurt all the time, but especially whenever he bent his elbow abruptly or when he tried to raise it over his head. He had trouble just straightening it out. There were ice packs, heat lamps, whirlpool baths and massages.

Johnny didn't try throwing the ball until late the next week. On Thursday he came out to practice and threw to Shula, but he had to quit after two or three tosses. On Friday he was no better. Rest, plenty of rest, that's what his arm needed, the doctors said.

Then Shula announced that I was to be the starting quarterback. "Unitas will miss the first three games," he told the team. "We'll be going with Earl."

CHAPTER TWENTY-TWO

The first game of the season was against San Francisco, and winning it was vital. We *had* to win; we had to show the rest of the league that the absence of Unitas wasn't going to hurt us.

The Forty-Niners were not going to be easy. The week before, in an exhibition game, they had lost to the Rams by only one point. They had a new coach in Dick Nolan and he had installed a tricky multiple offense. It figured that they were going to be "up" for the game. Our plan was to go out and control the ball, to move it. There was to be no fancy stuff, no attempts for any cheap touchdowns, just solid football.

In the hours before the game, I could feel the tension build. I knew it was up to me, that I was being depended upon. I could feel the butterflies; it was almost like I was a rookie. After all, nothing had happened in recent years to boost my confidence. The Giants had given up on me; Detroit had preferred someone else. And I hadn't won my present job; it had become mine by default. Maybe Sherman was right; maybe Gilmer was. I hadn't started a game for almost two years. Was I going to be rusty? Was I going to be able to handle the Colts' system? I knew I was going to have to concentrate more intensely than I ever had before. I had a lot of worries.

We kicked off. The Forty-Niners couldn't move the ball and had to punt.

I tried a pass to Matte that got us a first down. Then I went to Matte again. He was open. I threw. From out of nowhere came Roland Lakes, the huge tackle for the Forty-Niners, vaulting into the air, both arms upstretched. The ball struck him on the forearm and caromed off like a line drive from a baseball bat. I was flat-footed; I couldn't move. Stan Hindman, the other San Francisco end, had been blocked out and around the pocket by Sam Ball and he was in back of me. Well, the ball sailed right to him, hitting him in the pit of the stomach. He grappled with it for a second, then managed to clutch it to his chest, and the next thing I knew I was chasing him into the end zone.

Not two minutes had passed and we were a touchdown behind. "Oh, my God," I thought as I was running off the field. "Is it going to be one of those kind of games? Or worse, is it going to be one of those kind of *years?*"

The fans in Memorial Stadium make plenty of noise. They are probably the noisiest in the league. But after Hindman scored, the place got real quiet, no boos, just absolute silence, like everyone had gone home. Shula didn't say anything to me. No one did. They were all in a state of shock.

When we huddled after the kickoff, I said, "Let's go gang. We've got to get it back. Let's not get excited. Let's move down the field."

Our first drive flattened out, but the defensive team went out and got us the ball back. This time we moved beautifully. I handed to Jerry Hill and he found daylight a couple of times. Orr grabbed a pass and the play covered twenty-five yards. We were moving.

On the next play I called a pass with Ray Perkins to be the primary receiver. As I got set to throw, I saw a linebacker storming in. I knew this meant that two men would now be covering Perkins. I was supposed to switch-off to Mackey, the secondary receiver, but I didn't react quickly enough. I did notice that Perkins had cut very deep and behind one of the safeties, so I put the ball up high. He made a spectacular diving leap to get it, catching it on the 1 yard line and rolling into the end zone without a hand touching him. The official, however, put the ball down on the one. It didn't matter. Tom Matte scored on the next play. Lou Michaels' kick tied it.

When I came off the field and the crowd was cheering, I can't tell you how great it felt. The nightmarish memory of Hindman's freak interception was blotted out. We had met a fierce challenge, a crisis, and we had answered with a touchdown of our own. No one had panicked. No one had shown any anxiety during our drive. We knew what we had to do and we did it. Out of this test, I gained an even greater respect for the Colt team, and I'm sure they became more confident in me. It was an important turning point, not only in the game but for the entire season.

Our second touchdown gave me a big boost, too. It came in the second quarter at the end of a fifty-eight-yard drive. We had the ball on San Francisco's 8 yard line. It was third and one. Shula put in Tom Mitchell to line up tight at left end instead of splitting wide. John Mackey was set tight on the other side. The Forty-Niners, expecting a run, tightened their defense. This is what we had hoped for. I faked to Jerry Hill who slanted off left tackle. Then I pivoted away from the play action and tossed a feathery pass over the middle to Mitchell. He was wide open. He took it at the 3 yard line and bulled his way over a linebacker and into the end zone. The whole thing—the faking, the decoying and Mitchell's catch—worked to perfection. That gave us the lead and I knew we were ahead to stay.

We scored again in the third period when I hit Orr with a seventeen-yard pass. Two field goals accounted for the rest of the points. We won 27–10.

Our defensive team was great, just great. The only touchdown that the Forty-Niners got came as a result of Hindman's interception. They were constantly forcing Brodie's hand. At one stage in the second quarter, he was checking-off on every other play. And once John threw to Rick Volk, our safety, and there wasn't a San Francisco player within miles of him.

I got lots of help. Shula kept Jimmy Orr and Ray Perkins going in and out with plays. And in the huddle, Tom Matte would listen carefully to each of my calls to see if I was using the right numbers. He had to correct me four or five times. Once I called a reverse involving Mackey to the same side on which he was going to be lined up. Before I could unravel it, we were hit with a delay penalty. And whenever I'd go to the sidelines, I'd talk to Johnny, and he'd have suggestions on what receivers were open.

In the locker room after, the team voted me the game ball. God knows, they didn't do it because I had put on a skillful performance. I felt like I had made a million mistakes. They did it to show that I belonged. When I left the stadium that night, I felt twelve feet tall. It was going to be a great year. I just knew it was.

CHAPTER TWENTY-THREE

One of the newspapers in Baltimore had one of those inquiring photographer columns—it was called "Curious Camera"—and they sent this guy around the city asking, "Will Earl Morrall prove a winner for the Colts?" He got answers like, "Johnny Unitas is the greatest quarterback in pro football, and it would be a hard blow if the Colts had to go without him," and, "I don't want to even think that the Colts would have to win without Unitas." And one guy said flatly, "No, we can't possibly win with Earl Morrall."

The feeling was, I think, that I would prove competent. But as for winning the championship, they needed Unitas for that.

I tried not to pay any attention to what was being said or written, to take each game as it came. Atlanta was next. We were loose. You try not to let down for the weaker teams, but subconsciously you sometimes do. Shula kept after us all through the week, warning us of the perils of indifference.

The way the game started I thought we were going to win by fifty points. The first two times we got the ball we scored. Several times Matte and Hill got long yardage and they were really punishing the tacklers. Atlanta used a zone and I had no trouble reading the moves.

Then I think we got careless. There were some missed tackles that were costly, and I threw three interceptions, all of them in the second quarter. Atlanta got close, 14–10.

With less than a minute remaining in the second period,

Shula sent in one of the oldest plays in football—the "flea flicker." According to *The History of American College Football*, the flea flicker was introduced by Bob Zuppke in 1910 at Oak Park, Illinois, High School. In 1925, when Zuppke was coaching at Illinois, he used it against Penn in a game at Philadelphia. It's designated as "38 flow special" in the Baltimore playbook.

We had the ball on the Atlanta 46 and their defense was anticipating a run. The play started like a sweep with Matte carrying and guards John Williams and Glenn Ressler pulling out to lead. Before he turned downfield, Matte stopped abruptly and threw back to me. Meanwhile, Jimmy Orr had ambled downfield a few steps, then broken for the corner. When I got the ball from Matte, I saw Jimmy in the end zone all by himself. He was just standing there like he was waiting for a bus. In my hurry to get the ball to him, I threw without having a firm grip on the laces. The ball went high and soft as a result, and Jimmy had to come back a step or two to make the catch, but he scored easily. It was a great way to end the quarter.

The Falcons came back strong in the third period and made the score 21–20. We fumbled three times and that helped them.

It wasn't until the fourth quarter that we got into the clear. We had the ball on our own 14. It was second down and twenty-four and I called a pattern to Orr. Lee Calland, the Atlanta defender, had taken away the outside, so Jimmy threw him a fake and broke inside. My protection was perfect. I thought I overthrew the ball, but Jimmy made the grab at the Falcon 45 and wasn't brought down until he reached the 2. Matte scored on the next play.

We had come close to kicking it away. A topflight team would have killed us. The flea flicker is probably what

176

saved the day. It's the type of play on which you look very good or very bad. This time we looked good.

The next week we played the Steelers. They figured to be easy and they were. We had learned our lesson against Atlanta. There was no letting down and we made few mistakes. One of the day's highlights was another razzle-dazzle play sent in by Shula. This time it was a variation of the old Statue of Liberty play, with the halfback circling around in back of the quarterback and snatching the ball out of his upraised hand. Matte got fifteen yards with it. We won, 47–7.

Unitas was supposed to be ready to take over by this time, but he wasn't. He still had intense pain in his elbow. He threw sparingly, and when he did throw, he merely lobbed the ball. After the Atlanta game, Johnny's trouble was diagnosed to be more serious than tendonitis. The doctors found that he had ripped a section of muscle fibre in the inside of his forearm.

You could see he was hurting. Sometimes we'd alternate in the quarterback slot during practice. Johnny would step up and take the snap and get back quickly, just as he always had. But when he threw, you could see he wasn't able to snap off the ball. It was a little bit soft. It reminded me of some of the passes that I threw when I was recovering from my broken collarbone. They had a wobble. Some of the guys watching me would go, "Quack, quack, quack," because they said the ball looked like a duck in flight. But no one ever went "Quack, quack, quack" when Unitas threw.

Johnny had trouble throwing long, too. And once in a while you'd see him wince in pain. But he never said a word, never once.

The following week we played the Bears. They are always tough. They have more defensive plays than some teams have on offense. They love to blitz. The cornerbacks play bump-and-run. Curtis Gentry on one side, and Bennie McRae on the other, both very fast, pick-up the receivers at the line of scrimmage, and they do anything they can to knock them off stride, keeping practically nose to nose with them, while the line goes for the quarterback.

Gale Sayers was the No. 1 man in the Bears' offense, and he was averaging 5.95 yards per carry. He got loose for a fifty-nine-yard run in the second quarter to put the Bears out in front. But we came right back. I connected with Willie Richardson on a fifty-yard pass play that tied the score on the very next series.

A few minutes later the defense got us the ball again, and we went into a slot formation, with Willie Richardson and Jimmy Orr split wide to the right, and John Mackey to the left. I was to fake a handoff to Hill, then pass to Matte breaking down the right sideline. Well, when I went back to pass, I saw right away that Matte was surrounded. It looked as if the entire Bear team had diagnosed the play. I was under pressure now and I had to move. Then I spotted Mackey. No one was near him. I threw, leading him a little inside, and he grabbed the ball and started running. At the 10 yard line, Richie Petitbon slammed into him, but John wouldn't go down. He stumbled, but kept right on going, leaving Petitbon on the ground behind. Then Rosey Taylor grabbed one of Mackey's legs, but still John wouldn't stop. He was enraged now, and he kept pumping the free leg, and he stepped all over poor Taylor, on his chest, his head, his legs—everywhere. Finally Mackey jerked the other leg free and burst into the end zone. It was a perfect example of what strength and determination can do.

Not long after, we were on the sidelines, and Jimmy Orr told me that he could beat his man on a down-and-out pattern, what we call a "Q pattern." When we were going out on the field, Orr said, "Don't call it now (the ball was on our 9 yard line); wait until we get into their territory. I want to get a touchdown out of it."

When we got down to the Chicago 48, I called Jimmy's play. It was like he had a crystal ball. He brought his man into the middle, faked beautifully, then broke for the corner all by himself. All I had to do was get the ball out there.

We had a 21–7 lead at halftime. Seldom have the Bears been so thoroughly embarrassed in such a short span of time. The final was 28–7.

While all of our touchdowns had come about as the result of passes, the ground attack was a key factor. It had been in all of our earlier games, too. We were averaging about 140 yards rushing per game. A quarterback puts his own special stamp on a team, and the Colts were now beginning to reflect some of my thinking. I'm a firm believer in the importance of the running game. I like to establish it right at the outset, and I'm likely to emphasize it throughout the entire game. When I began doing this at Baltimore, it contrasted sharply with the way Johnny ran the team. He, of course, relied on the pass. He had not the slightest compunction about putting the ball in the air anytime and from any place on the field. And why not? He was incredibly gifted and more successful with the pass than any quarterback known.

The Colts depended on Johnny to bring them through in tight situations. In fact, they may have depended on him too much. He came up with the big play so often they got to expect him to, and as a result they may have eased up once in a while. But when I took over, I think many of the players realized that they were going to have to work harder, to really dig in. I'm less spectacular than Johnny. I'm less likely to throw the long pass when it's third and two. I'm less likely to break a game open. It's my nature to be conservative.

The stress on the running game typifies the way I like to run a team. I think my foremost skills as a quarterback are in faking the ball and play-calling. A running game makes the most of these attributes. Don't get me wrong; I like to pass and I've had good success as a passer, and, of course, you have to mix in passes to make the running game effective, but the whole idea of football is to move forward, and I prefer to do this by emphasizing the ground game.

When you put the accent on the ground game, you reap a number of beneficial side effects. Most linemen prefer running plays. It gives each one a chance to fire out and get his man. On a pass, your linemen have to either drop back or stand their ground and take the rush. So it's a matter of hitting or getting hit.

Running keeps the defensive players wary. They're not intent on merely trying to get to the passer. They have to be cautious. Is a runner coming out of the backfield? Is it a fake? Is it a pass? Each defensive man has to establish what's happening before he can make his move.

And when you run a good deal, you're in control. You're constantly wearing down the opposition. At the same time, your defensive team is resting on the sidelines. This can be extremely significant, especially in the late stages of a tight game.

In Baltimore, once the running game got more stress, it got stronger. Matte, Hill, and Mackey on the endarounds were the backbone of the ground attack. The more they were used the better they became.

Against the Bears, Jerry Hill had gotten ninety yards rushing. The defense knew that either Hill or Matte might come booming out of the backfield at any time and they weren't able to rely on the blitz as much. Before the Bears game, there was a lot of talk that this was going to be our first real test of the season, that the games we had played before Chicago were against pushover teams, so this was a big win. And it was a big game for me personally. I had fourteen completions in twenty-five attempts for 302 yards. It had been years since I had done anything like that.

The next week we played San Francisco again, and if you looked at the statistics, you couldn't help but get the impression that the Forty-Niners had won handily. They had twenty-eight first downs; we had eighteen. They had 392 total yards to our 278. They totaled 236 yards passing to our 182. They controlled the ball for seventy-seven offensive plays to our fifty-one.

Yet we beat them without too much trouble, 42-14.

What gave us the advantage was our ability to make the big play, to get the ball over the goal line whenever we got close. As in our first game with the Forty-Niners, the defense kept Brodie under pressure. He was intercepted three times.

Johnny made his first appearance of the season in this game. There were about eleven minutes remaining and we were leading, 28–17, when Shula sent him in. His passes lacked power and speed, but he compensated for it. He knew when to let go and he would hit the open spot. He got us two more touchdowns.

The trip back to Baltimore was torture. Friendship Airport was socked in by heavy fog when we arrived at about two A.M. Monday morning, and we had to go north to Newark to land. Then came a four-hour bus trip to get us back to Baltimore. Altogether, it took thirteen or fourteen hours. But I don't remember anyone complaining. When you're winning you can stand anything.

CHAPTER TWENTY-FOUR

The Coastal Division had settled down to a duel between ourselves and the Rams. Both of us had won five games without losing. We were scheduled to play the Rams in two weeks, but first there was a game with the Browns in Cleveland. Through the years the Colts have never seemed to do well against the Browns and this game didn't do anything to change the tradition.

We were slow and sluggish; we were flat. We couldn't get anything started. Our best plays lost yardage. The defense was as inept as the offense. They couldn't stop Leroy Kelly or Bill Nelsen's short passes. And a roughing the kicker and a roughing the passer penalty hurt us at critical times.

At halftime we were down, 14–7. Shula, in an effort to lift the team, decided to start Unitas in the third period. "We gotta do something," he said to me in the locker room. "I'm gonna send Johnny in. Let's see what he can do."

What could I say? Shula was the boss. I wanted to stay in. I wanted to be the one who would bring the team back. But—and maybe this is a weakness of mine—I could see Shula's viewpoint. He thought a change would give the team a boost. Perhaps he was right, so when he told me that he was assigning me to the bench, I kind of shrugged. I don't even remember what I said, but I know I didn't argue. But it tore me up inside.

Whatever it was that paralyzed the rest of us quickly struck Unitas, too. His passes were deflected or batted into the air to be picked off by the Browns, and they converted two of his tosses into touchdowns and a third into a field goal to put the game on ice.

Johnny was releasing the ball high and once, on a pass to Orr, he grabbed his elbow. When he came off the field, he would be muttering to himself and he kicked the turf in anger. He completed only one pass of the twelve he threw, and late in the game some of the fans began to boo. And we were playing at home! Fans are weird. I've heard them boo Y. A. Tittle in San Francisco and Joe Schmidt in Detroit. I've heard them boo all the best. And now Unitas. Johnny took the boos in stride. "You're a hero when you win," he said, "a bum when you lose. That's the game." That's the way most guys feel.

While we were losing to the Browns—the final was 30–20—the Rams were winning. We were now 5–1; they were 6–0. We couldn't afford another loss. Our upcoming meeting with them was a "must" game for us.

Shula gave me the starting assignment.

We tore them up.

If ever there was a day that belonged to the defense, this was it. The adrenalin really flowed. In the line Billy Ray Smith, Bubba Smith, Fred Miller and Ordell Braase smothered everything that came their way. Miller seemed to be in on almost every play. The linebackers—Mike Curtis, Dennis Gaubatz and Don Shinnick—played like they had written the Rams' game plan. They were always at the right place at the right time. Curtis was incredible. He made ten unassisted tackles. Ten! The cornerbacks and the deep men handled virtually everything that came their way. Five times Roman Gabriel was slammed down under the fierce pass rush.

You could see the stunned Ram linemen getting jolted

back. You could hear it. You could hear the sharp *thwacks* as leather hit leather, and the animal-like grunts. The Rams were forced into making one mistake after another.

I set up the first touchdown with a screen pass to Matte, the play covering fifty-five yards. Jerry Hill dived into the end zone from the 2. Curtis' bone crushing tackle separated Willie Ellison from the football on the first play after the kickoff, and Miller picked it up and sprinted thirty-two yards to the Rams' 4. Two plays later I went back to pass, saw a mile-wide hole to the right, and zipped through it for my first touchdown as a Colt.

When I came to the sidelines after the touchdown Johnny had a play for me. He had been talking with Jimmy Orr and Jimmy had told him that he could beat his man, Irv Cross, deep and into the middle. One problem was to get John Mackey through so that Ed Meador, the Rams' weak side safety, would pick him up, leaving Cross alone on Orr.

Right after the kickoff we got the ball back when Jerry Logan intercepted. I called the slant-in pattern that Johnny had suggested. We were on our own 44 yard line. When I went back to pass, I saw Meader go with Mackey. Orr got open, wide open. I fired. Touchdown!

That made three touchdowns in the space of five minutes. In the second half I passed for another, hitting Tom Mitchell. We coasted after that.

It was the first defeat for Los Angeles in seventeen games of regular season play. It showed them to be vulnerable. Shula said it was the season's turning point.

Maybe losing to the Browns was what we needed. It woke us up. We were a much different team against the Rams. We were to meet them again in the last game of the season. But no one was worried about them now, and some of the guys were beginning to think Super Bowl. I wasn't though. I was thinking about next week. We were playing the Giants in New York.

CHAPTER TWENTY-FIVE

Even though we had won it convincingly, the Los Angeles game was not one of my better performances of the year. I rushed my passes when I didn't have to, especially in the first half. The line gave me all the time in the world, more than I needed. But I'd step back there and—bang— I'd fire. I missed some I shouldn't have missed. I was intercepted three times.

But the following week when we played the Giants, I had a dream day. It was almost as if I had been saving myself for Allie Sherman. I called most of the game myself. My passes were consistently right on target. It was a confident, polished performance, my best as a Colt.

I got the running game started early. Jerry Hill made some nice gains, and Tom Matte picked up twenty-three yards off left tackle to set up a first period field goal.

I read the New York defenses as if I still had a copy of their playbook. In the second period I hit Willie Richardson and Jimmy Orr with touchdown passes less than four minutes apart. We led, 16–0, at the half.

Time after time I clicked on third down situations. On our final drive, which carried ninety-four yards, I connected with Ray Perkins for twenty-nine yards on a third-and-eighteen situation. I hit Mackey for ten yards when it was third down and we needed that much. And when it was third and nine on the Giants 40 yard line, I passed to Orr and he made it all the way to their 2. I was sixteen for twenty-four for the day.

In past games the Colt defense had often been bewildered

by Tarkenton's scrambling. But not this day. The rush line simply flowed with him, virtually abandoning the blitz. Braase and Bubba Smith, the ends, drove straight ahead, thus preventing Francis from rolling to the outside. Whenever one of the rush line was hit with a good block, he was instructed to ride it out, stay back, and keep alert to cut off Tarkenton's escape route. When Fran began to run around, each linebacker picked out a receiver and stayed with him. It was a frustrating day for Fran. He wasn't around at the end. Gary Wood finished up. The Giants didn't get past midfield during the first quarter, and the deepest they got all day was our 10. The final score was 26–0. It was the first time the Giants had been shut out in seventy-six games.

As the game reached its final stages, the huge crowd at Yankee Stadium began chanting, "Good-by, Allie," and some fans in the end zone unfurled a big banner that read, "Earl Wasn't Good Enough for Allie."

One reporter said after that I played the game with a smile on my face. I could have. It was a sweet day.

CHAPTER TWENTY-SIX

We had beaten three of my former teams now, and the next week I came back to haunt the Lions. It was my first appearance in Detroit since Harry Gilmer had given me my walking papers more than three years before.

I wanted to have a good day—and I did. Jimmy Orr did, too, setting up two touchdowns with his catches. On one, Jimmy started inside, then broke outside, giving an extra fake to Dick LeBeau. When I threw, I couldn't see Jimmy; he was screened out by someone. But I had his moves down so well by this time that I knew where he was going to be. And it worked out. The play covered fifty-four yards.

Again our defense played a fierce game. In the fourth quarter, when we had a slim 27–10 lead, the Lions threatened. Bill Munson went back to pass, rolled out, then cocked his arm. But before he could get the ball away, Fred Miller slammed into him from behind, and buried Munson's nose in the ground.

Munson burst into anger and started screaming. Miller just laughed. "Keep quiet," he told Munson. "I'll be back to see you again in about four seconds." And he was. He put Munson down on the very next play. We took over the ball after another play and then ran out the clock.

We beat the Cardinals the next week and I threw three touchdown passes, quite an achievement because the Cards have a tough defense. Larry Wilson, their free safety, is the best in the business. He's all over the field making tackles and breaking up plays. He never stops hustling to get near the football. He's rugged and he hits hard. Early in the game I called a pass to Matte, but he broke earlier than I expected and so I was late with the ball. Wilson roared in, springing high, to intercept.

For the rest of the day I ran most of the plays out of a double wing. Hill was set just behind me, and Matte outside left tackle and about a yard back. Mackey was the strong side end; Willie Richardson was wide. Jimmy Orr was at left end. This kept the Cards in a man-to-man coverage. Wilson's responsibility was our halfback—Matte —and no one else.

Not long after we started with the double wing, I hit Willie with a pass and the play went for seventy-nine yards and a touchdown. Later Willie scored on a twenty-nine-yard pass play. The final was 27–0.

We set back the Vikings, 21–9, the next week. The game turned on a play late in the second quarter. We had the ball on the Minnesota 39 and it was third and three. I faked to Hill, then faked to Mackey who was running a slant-out. There was a defensive mixup and both the cornerback and the strong side safety moved to cover Mackey. This left Willie Richardson unguarded near the sideline, an easy target. He could have walked in. The Falcons fell the next week, 44–0.

The defense now had three shutouts for the season and they had given up only two touchdowns in the last six games. But while we were piling win upon win, so were the Rams. Our record was now 11–1–0; theirs was 10–1–1. Two weeks of the season remained. We were in a slightly better position than the Rams, but we couldn't afford to stumble.

We went out to Green Bay the next week. The Packers were fighting desperately to stay in the Central Division race.

There was some talk that Green Bay wasn't quite as tenacious in 1968 as they had been in previous years, that there was something lacking. Well, it was only newspaper talk. I never heard it from anyone who faced them on the playing field. No one on the Colts took them lightly, I know. They still had Dave Robinson, Ray Nitschke and Lee Roy Caffey as linebackers and anytime you have to face a trio like that you're in for a tough day.

The game's only touchdown came the second time we got possession. Mike Curtis had thrown a vicious tackle at Donny Anderson, separating him from the ball, and Bobby Boyd recovered on their 28.

Terry Cole slanted off tackle for two yards. On the next play, I called a pattern sending Willie Richardson deep. Nitschke and Robinson were red dogging, but Bill Curry and Terry Cole picked them up, so I had time. Herb Adderly was waiting for Willie, then went with him stride for stride, but Willie gave Adderly a beautiful fake and turned Herb around. I threw high, trying to get the ball over Adderly. I figured it was going to be Willie's or nobody's. Willie, leaping up, made the catch of the year to get it. That put us ahead, 7–0.

The Packers came right back with a field goal. But that was all the scoring they did. We won, 16–3.

The game virtually eliminated Green Bay from championship contention, and as the Packers were leaving the field for the locker room, the public address announcer implored the crowd: "How about an ovation for the Packers? They've given us some great football over the years." The fans gave a loud cheer and they waved small American flags that had been given out at the gate. But the whole thing struck me as being a bit uncalled for. I don't know why everyone is so anxious to write off the Packers. I think every newspaper in the country has run at least one "end of an era" story concerning the team. But Green Bay will be back, and soon.

We beat Green Bay on a Saturday and the next day the Rams were scheduled to meet the Bears. Well, they were upset, 17–16, and that made us the Coastal Division champions. The following week we beat them in the final game of the season—the score was 28–24.

The next hurdle was the Western Conference championship and to win it we had to beat the Minnesota Vikings, winners of the Central Division. This time we would be playing the Vikings at Memorial Stadium. Playing at home can be an important factor. I always seem to do better among friends. There's something comfortable about playing in your own stadium. It's like being in a room in your own home; there's something secure about it, a feeling you never get from a room in anyone else's house, even the house of a close friend. It can even be the same type of house. But it's different; it's not yours. And when you're playing at home and you begin to move the team, you hear the encouragement and feel the excitement. All this helps.

The Vikings were a rugged defensive team. They had a big, rough front four—Carl Eller, Alan Page, Jim Marshall and Gary Larsen—who had contributed as much to the team's success as the Vikings' offense. Minnesota had also achieved good results by taking out an outside linebacker and replacing him with a defensive back. They did a lot of stunting with an added back or they doubled up on the outside receivers. And in a game against the Redskins, the Vikings had taken out all three linebackers and put defensive backs in. Whenever Jurgensen went back to pass, he usually had plenty of time, but there was no one to throw to. Almost every guy was double covered. They beat the Redskins badly. When we played the Vikings earlier in the season, we found them to be tough defensively. They kept us stymied in the second half; we didn't score a point.

We installed a new pass pattern for the game, one that we hadn't shown too much through the season. It was a sideline pattern with the receiver—Richardson or Orr—breaking down and then back and toward the sideline. From the films, we knew that they counted on their linebackers a great deal in defensing against passes, and we figured this pattern would pull the covering linebacker out of position and open up the whole outside. It did.

The first half was bitterly fought. Their rush line flattened me on the first play of the game and on at least three other occasions before halftime. To thwart the rush, I started faking to the fullback and rolling out behind him, and we used this strategy to score our first touchdown. It was late in the second quarter and we were on our own 25. We lined up in a slot formation with Richardson inside Orr, the split end. I took the snap and rolled to the right with Richardson my target. Karl Kassulke, the Vikings' free safety, stepped in to try to intercept, but he missed the ball and Willie caught it and took off. He got thirty-nine yards.

I called the same play again on the next down. This time Willie curled inside Kassulke and grabbed the ball with a diving catch to give us a first down on their 3. Two plays later I connected with Mitchell in the end zone. It was only his seventh pass reception of the season but his fifth touchdown.

We broke their backs in the third quarter. The second time we got the ball, I looped a pass over their linebacker to John Mackey who had found the open seam between the zones. When he made the catch, Mackey turned and smashed through two Minnesota safeties and then sprinted for the end zone. It was a forty-nine-yard play.

Joe Kapp, the Minnesota quarterback, played a whale of a game. It seemed like our line got a piece of him on almost every play. At the end he was bruised, battered, and covered with mud and I'll bet he ached until Easter.

But they didn't break him. Once, after stomping Kapp, Ordell Braase extended a hand to help him up. Kapp just ignored it.

Not long after Mitchell's touchdown, Kapp went back to pass and someone hit him, and the ball popped into the air and Mike Curtis picked it off. Curtis played fullback at Duke and he ran like one—sixty yards for a touchdown. That made it 21–0 and just about clinched things. The final was 24–14.

One day very late in the season—I think it was right after the Los Angeles game—I went down to the Colts' office for a meeting with the coaches. Don McCafferty was the first one I saw.

"Congratulations, Earl," he said.

"For what?"

"You've been named NFL Player of the Year. We just got the call from the league office."

Then Shula came in and he congratulated me too.

The news kind of took my breath away. If the poll had been taken early in the season, when I was still languishing in New York, I'm sure I wouldn't have gotten a single vote. My name wouldn't even have made the ballot.

The Player of the Year award was only the beginning. I also won the Jim Thorpe Trophy as the outstanding player in the NFL, an award given annually by the Newspaper Enterprise Association on the basis of a poll of the players. United Press International named me as the quarterback on their All Star team. And there were more, many more.

After I had been named NFL Player of the Year, someone asked Joe Schmidt of the Lions what he thought of the selection. "Great," he said, "just great. It's about time something nice happened to Earl."

I couldn't agree more.

But we still had to play the Cleveland Browns for the league title. Without the championship all the awards would be pretty meaningless.

CHAPTER TWENTY-SEVEN

The Browns, as the only team to have beaten us all year, had us worried. Our front rush line knew that they were going to have to bottle up Leroy Kelly, who had ended the season as the league's leading rusher. Bill Nelsen, the Browns' quarterback, loomed as a bigger obstacle. He seldom set up in conventional fashion, but simply darted back a step or two, raised his arm and fired, targeting on a receiver breaking to the sideline or across the middle. That was the way he beat the rush. Of course, the constant threat of Kelly also worked to discourage the rush.

Shula put in a few new wrinkles for the game. In the films, we had noticed that the Cleveland strong side safety always lined up on the same side as Mackey, while the free safety went to the other side. So we came up with a formation in which Mackey stationed himself right behind me, a variation of the I. I'm sure that Cleveland was disconcerted by it.

Another formation called for Orr and Richardson to split wide to the left, and Mackey right. We had used this during the season on pass plays, but for the Browns we planned to use it to trigger Matte on a sweep, with Mackey blocking out the defensive end.

Draw plays were another feature of the game plan. One of them featured trap blocks, our center taking out the Browns' left tackle, our right guard trapping their right tackle, and our left guard firing through to block out their middle linebacker. And either Matte or Hill would be right behind.

It was cold and the sky was leaden when we came out for the warmups. And it stayed cold all day, with a stiff wind off the lake that made it feel like zero.

The first quarter was scoreless, but as it was drawing to a close, we began to move the ball smartly. I hit Orr on the left side for fourteen yards. Two plays later, Richardson got clear and I connected with him for thirteen yards. Then, with the Browns looking for more passes, I switched to the ground game. Matte got six yards and twelve yards on successive slants, and then I sent Hill up the middle for three yards. We bogged down on the Cleveland 21 yard line and had to settle for a field goal, but it felt good to get that zero off the scoreboard.

The next time we got the ball I thought we'd go all the way. The drive started on our own 40. With Orr and Richardson set to the left, I sent Mackey around left end and he got ten yards. Then Hill hit left guard for four yards. Then three consecutive passes clicked—to Matte for two yards, to Mackey for eight, and to Orr on the left sideline for nineteen. We were rolling. I went back to the ground. Four plays later, Matte scored from one yard out, hitting off left tackle and flipping over backward into the end zone.

After the kickoff, the Browns moved almost as far as midfield when Nelsen, passing deep to Milt Morin, saw Rich Volk intercept and run the ball to the Cleveland 42. On first down I called an end sweep with Hill carrying and he got about two yards. We called time and I hustled to the sidelines to talk to Shula. In watching the films during the week, we had noticed that when Mackey lined up on the weak side of the slot formation, the Cleveland linebacker on that side paid little or no attention to him. So we had put in a screen pass to take advantage of this lapse. I wanted to use it now. Shula was thinking the same thing. "Use the screen to Mackey," he said when I came up to him.

The play was a gem. Mackey took the ball and streaked to the Cleveland 14, but he fumbled. Erich Barnes recovered and worked his way to the 23. There were two minutes left in the half.

On the next play our defense couldn't have been better. Nelsen, hoping for a long gain, went back to pass and looked for a sideline receiver, but every man was covered. The front four came blowing in and Nelsen tried to throw the ball away, over the sideline. But just as he let go he was hit, and the ball hung. Mike Curtis rushed over to make the interception and his momentum carried him out of bounds.

It was first and ten on the Cleveland 33. Only about a minute and a half remained.

Naturally, the Browns were looking for a pass. And when I took the snap and started to rollout, every defenseman went to his pass coverage, but I slipped the ball to Matte and he roared straight up the middle for twelve yards. I called another draw on the very next play, sending Hill up the middle. No one was looking for it. I thought he was going all the way but he was stopped at the Cleveland 12.

There was still a full minute left. We didn't have to hurry. I stayed on the ground, calling Matte on an off-tackle slant. Tom started inside, then cut outside behind a fine block thrown by Jimmy Orr. He just managed to keep his balance as he swept into the end zone.

We had a 17–0 lead when we went into the locker room, but no one thought we had the game won. Shula warned us against letting down. "We're not going to sit on this lead," he told the team. "We're going to add to it. Play like the score is nothing to nothing." When we went back out on the field, we were determined to play aggressively, to dominate. We felt that a long run by Kelly or a Nelsen pass—any spark that might ignite the Browns—could turn the game around.

The Browns kicked off but we couldn't move the ball. Dave Lee came in for the first time to punt. Cleveland took over and were forced to try for a field goal from their 43. It went wide but we were offside, so they got another chance. This went wide, too.

We failed to move the ball again, and now it was beginning to bother us. We had the lead, yes, but we couldn't play our normal ball control game. We couldn't get the upper hand.

Our defense went out and got us the ball again. This time we got something going. On third and six, I connected with Tom Mitchell for a first down on the Cleveland 44. Then I tried Mackey on an end-around, but he was dropped for a loss. I figured that on the next play Erich Barnes, the Cleveland cornerback, would be playing fairly shallow, looking for a pass that would get us a first down. We needed sixteen yards. My plan was to have Willie Richardson slip behind Barnes, and I called a pattern sending Willie deep.

But Barnes crossed me up. He played way off, making Willie come to him. When Willie got to Barnes, he kept right on flying, and Erich had to turn and go with him. I threw, trying to keep the ball high and close to the sideline, but I failed to get the distance I wanted. Willie stopped, turned, and came back a step or two, then out-fought Barnes to make the grab. It was sensational. Willie was brought down on the 5 yard line. Two plays later Matte slammed into the end zone for his third touchdown of the day. Michaels' kick gave us a 24–0 lead. It was late in the third quarter. We knew we had them.

The defense hadn't played a better game all year long. They shut off Kelley. They didn't make any big changes, but simply read the formations better than they had in our first meeting. And when the Browns couldn't run, Nelsen started throwing, and then the rush line increased the pressure on him, and they stopped the passing game too. Only twice did the Browns get into our territory, and never deeper than the 33 yard line. As for the offensive line, well, no one laid a hand on me all day long.

You could feel the exuberance surge through the guys as they stood on the sidelines. We scored a field goal and later another touchdown, but they were just icing on the cake. After Richardson's tremendous catch and the touchdown that followed, we knew we had it won. There, on the sidelines, we had to hide our delight, but everyone had this inner joy. Whenever my eyes met someone else's you could tell it. There were the wide grins, the confident nods. And there was great satisfaction, too, because not only had we won but we had played like champions, almost flawless football.

After we had scored the last touchdown and I came off the field, Unitas was there. He shook my hand.

"Congratulations, Earl," he said, and he was smiling. He really meant it. "It was a great season for you—and you deserved it."

A few minutes later the game ended and Johnny and I walked together to the locker room. We didn't say two words. We didn't have to. Each one of us knew what the other was thinking.

Inside, before they let the press in, we all bowed our heads for a minute. Some guys stood, others knelt, and Shinnick led us in the Lord's Prayer. And after, there was no dumping champagne on guys and no tossing coaches in the shower. None of that. Sure, we were happy. But this was a team that had a job to do. And they went out and did it.

I had always hoped that sports would provide me with moments like these. It made up for the frustration at San

Francisco and Pittsburgh, the long unfulfilling years at Detroit, and ignominy in New York. It made up for the broken wrist and the smashed collarbone, for the agonizing hot summer afternoons in places like Fairfield, Connecticut, and Birmingham, Michigan. It made up for plenty.

That night we flew back to Baltimore and there was a party at Johnny's restaurant, the Golden Arm. The crowd of fans outside were more jubilant than the players. The guys were happy, but there was this feeling of relief more than anything else, relief that the season was over at last, relief that the pressure was off.

During the party, several people asked me, "How do you think you'll do against the Jets?" They had won the American League title the same day, nosing out the Oakland Raiders.

The Jets? They were an unknown quantity. I had never seen them play, except maybe two or three times on television. I hadn't thought much about them. All I knew was that right now we were the champions. I wanted to enjoy that for a while. I had waited thirteen years to. I wasn't going to worry about the Jets. Not yet.

CHAPTER TWENTY-EIGHT

In the week before the Super Bowl, every time I picked up a newspaper or saw a television sports show, all I read or heard was what a great team we had and how we were going to bury the Jets.

Our defensive team was said to be among the best ever in the National League, if not *the* best. After all, hadn't they matched the fewest-points-allowed mark of 144 set by the Chicago Bears during the 1963 season? Hadn't they led the NFL by allowing only sixteen touchdowns all year, and only nine touchdowns on passes? Hadn't they shut out the Giants, Cards, Falcons, and Browns?

We were said to be much superior to the two Green Bay Super Bowl champions. How could the Jets possibly contend with such a team? The Las Vegas oddsmakers made us eighteen-point favorites, and of the hundreds of newspaper men that journeyed to Miami to cover the game, all but a small handful picked us to win.

So it would have been easy for us to have taken the Jets lightly. But we didn't. I'm sure of that.

The Colts had the incentive a team needs in order to win. "This is the hungriest team I ever saw," John Mackey declared. And he said it *after* the Cleveland game. That's how everyone on the team felt.

Another thing; we came away from the film sessions with great respect for the Jets. They were a sound team; they made very few mistakes.

I spent most of my time in the week before the game studying the Jet defenses, of course, and I developed a high regard for their linebackers—Ralph Baker on the left side, Al Atkinson in the middle, and Larry Grantham on the right. The Jets depended on their linebackers—Atkinson, especially—to get deep into the secondary and help out the safeties. In turn, this enabled the safeties to work more closely with the cornerbacks.

Their front four—end Gerry Philbin and tackle Paul Rochester on the left side, and end Verlon Biggs and tackle

John Elliott on the right—were quick and mobile, something like Green Bay's front four. Elliott impressed us the most. He could get off a block and pursue and he sort of reminded you of Henry Jordan of the Packers. Philbin had similar skills. Biggs, at six-foot-four and 268, was the biggest man in the line. Both he and Rochester were bulls, almost always boring straight in.

An important feature in our game strategy was our plan to key on the middle linebacker. The way he moved would dictate who I'd throw to. If he moved right, I'd throw left, and vice versa. We also planned to use draw plays in the early stages to keep their linebackers up tight, to prevent them from going deep to harass our receivers.

We kicked off and Earl Christy brought the ball out to the Jets 23 yard line. After picking up one first down, the Jets had to punt and we took over on our own 27.

The first few plays were beautiful. I hit Mackey with a flare and he ran over two Jets and made nineteen yards. Then Matte swept right end for another ten. Hill got seven. A few plays later I passed to Tom Mitchell for fifteen yards and we had a first down on the New York 19. The game plan was working perfectly. It looked like we were going to move right in.

On first down, I called a short, quick pass to Willie Richardson. We lined up in a slot formation, with Jimmy Orr out wide to the right and Willie in the slot. John Mackey was on the left side. Willie's pattern was a short diagonal to the right. I saw him break. I cocked my arm to fire. But at the last second Willie's man—I think it was Jim Hudson—rushed up to cover him. I had to hold up the throw. In another second one of the Jets came crashing in and I had to roll out to escape. Meanwhile, Willie had broken down the sideline and was in the clear. I figured he would continue straight down and I unloaded, leading him with the ball. But at almost the exact minute I threw, Willie broke to the left where he saw a wide hole. When he looked for the ball, he realized it was behind him and he had to stop, turn and go back. He managed to get a hand on it but it slipped from his grasp. This was a critical play. Had Willie and I connected, the worst we would have had was a first down inside the Jets five yard line. But no one paid much attention to this error in judgment at the time. After all, it was a first-down play, and it was very early in the game.

Two more pass attempts followed. On second down, Tom Mitchell was the intended receiver. He seemed to delay his break and I underthrew him. Tom dove for the ball but couldn't come up with it. On third down, the Jets came up with a perfect defensive call. Every receiver was covered. Matte was out in the flat and he had a linebacker with him. I thought I might be able to get the ball to Tom. But before I could unload, I was smothered, going down right on the line of scrimmage.

Then Lou Michaels came into try the field goal. He booted from the 27 yard line. The ball went wide to the right.

Looking back, I realize that our failure to score in this drive was very significant. It gave the Jets an emotional lift. It bolstered their confidence.

About four minutes remained in the quarter. The Jets took over the ball. Namath's passes got the team a first down, but on the next sequence they had to punt again.

We took over on our own 42. On first down I called a play that was meant to take advantage of the fact that the Jet linebackers liked to help out in the secondary. I sent Orr and Richardson fairly deep and held Mackey back, as if he were going to block. Mackey's man, Al Atkinson, their middle linebacker, saw the receivers streak down and saw Mackey crouch to block. As I peddled back, I saw Atkinson clear out to cover. Then Mackey broke, cutting across the middle two or three yards beyond the line of scrimmage. Atkinson veered back, but he was too late. I let go. It was right to Mackey—and he dropped it.

I have seen John Mackey catch passes off his shoe tops, and leap in the air like a high-jumper to grab them. I have seen him take the ball while his body is going through snake-like contortions. If ever there was a receiver who was worthy of the tag "glue-fingered," it is Mackey. When Mackey dropped that ball, it was like seeing Al Kaline flub an easy fly ball in right field, or watching Pancho Gonzales pound a lob right into the net. Those things don't happen.

On the next play I handed off to Jerry Hill who got three yards over the middle. Now it was third and seven. I decided to go with a long pass and again the Jets defended perfectly. Johnny Sample, the Jets left cornerback, was playing Richardson real deep and loose, letting Willie come to him. I could see Willie was going to have trouble, but when I threw I kept the ball high, hoping that Willie would be able to leap and get it. He's strong and he's done it many times. They went up together and Sample knocked the ball away. He made a good play. Dave Lee then punted and the ball rolled dead on New York's 4 yard line.

We got a big break a few minutes later, just seconds before the second quarter began. The Jets had the ball third and one on their own 13. Namath passed, hitting George Sauer with a quick sideline pop that looked like an easy first down. But Lenny Lyles smashed into Sauer from behind and jarred the ball loose. Ron Porter recovered for us on the Jets' 12.

Hill picked up a yard at left tackle, and then Matte turned left end and was brought down on the New York 6, a gain of seven yards.

If the game had a turning point, I'm sure it was the next play. It was third and four; we were on the Jets' 6. Shula sent in Tom Mitchell, our six-foot-two, 235-pound tight end. Often during the season we had used Mitchell in short yardage situations like this one. He's big and strong and able to shield away defenders with his body. We went into a double wing and put Mitchell wide to the left. Randy Beverly would be covering him.

Tom Matte and Jerry Hill were to decoy. Matte, also set to the left, was to slant left, taking the safety with him. Hill was to draw off the right linebacker. Mitchell was to run a quick slant-in, the idea being to get inside Beverly. Then I was to throw low, to Mitchell's belly, so he could clutch the ball to his body and fall to the ground in the end zone.

As I called out the signals, I could see that the Jet line had shifted to the right, and Al Atkinson, the middle linebacker, had moved a step or two to the left. I knew this meant he would be flying to the left, opposite to the direction Mitchell would be traveling. "Beautiful," I thought, "just beautiful."

It went great. Matte cleared his man out. So did Hill. And Mitchell threw a perfect fake at Beverly and then slipped inside him. I threw—hard. Mitchell had his arms open and waiting. The throw was right on target. Then suddenly the ball veered off course. Atkinson had tipped it, bending its path upward slightly so that it struck Mitchell on the shoulder. And then it caromed high into the air, straight up, just like a foul tip. Ironically, Beverly, the man who had been so thoroughly feinted out of position, became the hero. He turned, went back a step or two, and was under the ball when it came down to make an end-zone interception.

This was a big play. The Jets had stopped our touchdown drive, and now they took over the ball. The whole complexion of the game was reversed in those few seconds.

I couldn't believe our luck could be so bad. "What's happening?" I thought to myself as I came off the field. "What do we have to do?" And as I stood on the sidelines watching Namath call plays, I could see that the Jets were fired up. The crowd could, too, and their allegiance had shifted. When the teams had come out for the pre-game warmups, the Colts got the cheers, while the Jets, Namath in particular, had received loud boos. That changed. Now it was the Jets who were the heroes, the dragonslayers, and the massive crowd was rooting for them. I had hardly heard the fans before, but now the stands seemed to be in ceaseless tumult, one roar blending with the next, and you could feel the electricity, and I'm sure all this worked to exhilarate the Jets.

Namath led a brilliant counterattack, bringing the Jets eighty yards to a touchdown in twelve plays, two of which deserve mention. The Jets had the ball second and ten on their 48. We had a blitz on, but Namath saw it coming and fired to Sauer, a play that got them fourteen yards. Lenny Lyles was on Sauer but he couldn't get a hand in front of him. On the very next play, Namath came back to Sauer with a quick short-out pattern. We were expecting it and our defense was ready, and this time Lyles did get in front of Sauer. Namath unloaded anyway—but the ball slipped right through Lenny's fingers and Sauer grabbed it for an eleven-yard pickup. If Lyles could have held on to that ball, I'm almost certain we would have had a touchdown. He was well in front of Sauer and only Namath was between Lenny and the goal line and Lenny is very fast. But we just weren't able to make that kind of a play.

Two plays later Namath set up a Jet touchdown with a swing pass to Snell that covered twelve yards, giving the Jets first and goal on our 9 yard line. Snell then got five yards off right tackle, and followed by turning left end for the touchdown. Naturally, this increased the Jets' momentum. They had stopped us and, more important, had followed with a splendid drive that put them ahead, 7–0. If anyone on that team had been entertaining any doubts about their ability to win, their doubts were gone. The Jets were rolling.

The pressure was all on us now. We had to show that we could move the ball. We had to get some points. Preston Pearson brought the kickoff out to our 28. I missed Willie on a pass, but on the next play I connected with Matte who made a fine move on his defender to get clear. The play covered thirty yards and we were in Jet territory.

Two running plays got us only four yards. This hurt. I called a short pass with Orr the primary receiver. I was about to let go when I spotted Mackey in the clear. "This is where we get even," I thought. I went to Mackey and I think I may have hurried the throw. It was off to the right, but John made a terrific play, turning, sort of pirouetting, to come back and get his hands on it. Johnny Sample was playing my eyes, and he left Willie Richardson on the outside and came flying over to Mackey. Poor John. Because I had thrown to the right, he never really got a chance to put the ball away, and when Sample crashed into him from the blind side, the ball spurted away. In various accounts of the game, the play is listed as an "incomplete pass." But it was much more than that. It was another big play, another missed opportunity. At this point our only play was a field goal. Michaels kicked from the 46 yard line. Again the ball went wide to the right.

On the next series, Namath mixed his plays nicely and got the Jets to within field goal range, but Jim Turner missed.

When we took over the ball, there were about four minutes remaining in the half. I hit Willie for six yards. On the next play I handed to Matte who broke Jim Hudson's tackle at the line of scrimmage and streaked fifty-eight yards before Butch Baird brought him down from behind. Just before the play ended, Sample jumped on Matte and gave him a knee in the back. Matte leaped to his feet and started for Sample with his fists but some other players broke it up.

At any rate, we had a first down on the Jets' 16 yard line—another golden chance. After Jerry Hill got a yard off tackle, I called a pass play with Willie Richardson the primary receiver—and I blew it. Willie broke toward the middle, but when I unloaded, I threw behind him. He managed to reach back and get one hand on the ball. However, Johnny Sample, who was racing back to plug the gap, got *both* hands on it and held on, falling to the ground at the 2 yard line.

Our defense held the Jets and they had to punt. We took over on the New York 42 with forty-three seconds remaining. I threw a screen pass to Jerry Hill that got us a yard. Now there were only twenty-five seconds left, time for one more play. Shula wanted the flea flicker, the same play we had used successfully against the Falcons earlier in the season.

It started out fine. I handed off to Matte who was heading right. He stopped, turned, and lateraled back to me, his pass covering about twenty yards. When we worked the play against Atlanta, the ball came back high and I had to jump to get it, but this time it was low, about belt high, and I had to turn to my right to make the catch. When I looked for a receiver, there was Jerry Hill racing down the middle. He had plenty of room so I just sort of arched the ball instead of throwing hard. It floated—giving Jim Hudson, the Jets' safety, enough time to race over and make an interception.

The gun went off ending the half. I ran for the locker room. I felt miserable. If I had just run with the ball, I could have gotten us into field goal position. And then Boyd told me about Orr being wide open. I felt worse.

Sure, we were down when we filed into the locker room, but we were still confident we were going to win. I'm sure of that. There was no despair. After all, we had moved the ball well. We had made yardage. What we hadn't done was make the plays we needed most.

The fact that we hadn't scored was tough for me to take. In every game I play, I have a tremendous compulsion to get that zero off the scoreboard. It really haunts me. Two points, three points—anything—is a sign that you're moving forward, a sign of success. But that goose egg up there represents failure, and when you're the quarterback you feel it more deeply than anyone else.

I tried to wipe from my mind all the things that had gone wrong—the botched pass to Willie, the ball that Mackey had dropped, Beverly's fluke interception, the ball that had slipped through Lyles' fingers, the missed field goals and the muffed flea flicker. God, it was a long list.

If any single one of these had gone our way, the game would have been turned around. The whole thing was incredible, like some evil dream. I marveled at the fact that the Jets weren't two or three touchdowns ahead, not just one.

Shula started to talk and he was hot. I had seen him like this only a couple of times before, once during the Atlanta game that we almost gave away, and again when we played Cleveland during the regular season, a game we ultimately lost.

"We're making mistakes; we're stopping ourselves," he said, and then he paused and glared at us to let the words sink in. "You've got them believing in themselves. You've got them believing they're better than we are." It lasted three or four minutes.

We were buoyed up when we went back out onto the field. We felt sure things were going to be different.

But the third quarter tore us up.

What we intended to do was play sound football, merely to move the ball. No one had panicked; nothing bizarre was planned. The first play was to be a run with Matte carrying. I handed to Tom. He knifed through left tackle. And fumbled. The Jets recovered.

This was a jolt. I think it dented our confidence more than anything that happened before. We could see the pattern of the first half beginning to repeat itself, and our poise and assurance began to drain away, little by little, like beans trickling out the bottom of a torn sack. It was sad.

Namath got the Jets as deep as our 11 yard line, but then on successive plays Boozer and he were hit for losses. On fourth down Turner booted a field goal to put New York ahead, 10–0.

The next time we got the ball the team was flat. I overthrew Mackey. Then I hit Jerry Hill with a short flare, but there was no gain. On third down I called a delayed pattern to Mackey, but two men had him covered. I had to scramble. They brought me down. I lost two yards.

Shula was waiting for me as I came off the field. "I'm going to put Johnny in," he said. "I'm going to give him a try. We've got to get rolling." I nodded, that's all. I remembered back to the Cleveland game earlier in the year. The team was flat and Shula had put Unitas in to start the third quarter. I had really boiled. But not this time, it wasn't nearly so hard to take. If I was a coach and my team was being quarterbacked by a guy who couldn't seem to get the ball over the goal line, I'd sure as hell do something. I'd send my wife in if I thought it would help. Shula really had little choice. I hoped Johnny could get the club back on the track, maybe salvage something out of the tragedy that was being written.

Namath was bringing the Jets down the field again and the crowd was urging him on, but I hardly noticed what was happening. I paced the sidelines and over and over I kept asking myself what had gone wrong. There never once had been a day like this all season long; never before had we gotten close and not gotten in. I thought about the long sessions with the coaches during the previous week, and the extra time the receivers and I had spent practicing, and I thought about the game plan and how carefully it had been developed. And it had worked. We did roll up good yardage. We just couldn't make the big play.

I think I have good staying power, that I'm able to keep confident when the obstacles seem big or when the breaks go against the team. But throughout all my professional career I couldn't recall a day like this one, where one piece of bad fortune kept piling upon another. I kept saying to myself, "Don't let it get you down." In time, I'm sure the Colts would have started clicking, but football is a game, and like any game it has certain time limits. The afternoon grew darker and the scoreboard, flashing away the seconds one by one, came to dominate the scene. I began to feel that we just weren't meant to win, that the whole thing was preordained.

At first Unitas had trouble moving the team, but midway in the fourth quarter he got us into the end zone, the touchdown coming at the end of a fourteen-play, eighty-yard drive. We tried an onside kick and it worked, with Mitchell recovering on the Jets 44. There was hope. Unitas completed two passes that got us a first and ten on the Jets' 24. There were about three minutes left.

Johnny hit Richardson for five yards, but then missed three passes in a row. As Johnny said later, a quarterback has to play to stay sharp and he hadn't been playing. We got possession one more time. But there were only seconds left and we couldn't score. It ended 16–7.

"Can Earl Morrall do it?"

I think a lot of people asked themselves that question at the beginning of the season when the Giants traded me to the Colts and I had to step in for Unitas. But it was a question I never had to ask myself. I was sure I could.

CHAPTER TWENTY-NINE

The 1969 Super Bowl is the No. 1 subject people want to talk about when they see me. Whenever I make a banquet appearance, appear on television or radio, make a sales call, or just go to church on Sunday morning, I never fail to be asked what happened that gray Sunday afternoon at the Orange Bowl. I have a feeling it's going to be that way for the rest of my life.

One by one, I'll answer the questions that I'm asked most often.

Was it a handicap for the Colts to prepare for a team they had never faced before?

Not at all. After all, the teams we play over the regular season are all "new" teams to some degree. From year to year, players change and sometimes coaches, too, so you're always facing personnel and playing situations you haven't seen before. It's always a matter of preparing on a week-to-week basis, and so getting ready for the Jets wasn't really anything different for us.

We had six or seven Jets game films (and they had a similar number of ours). The coaches analyzed the films carefully, charting the frequency with which they used each of their various offensive and defensive formations and in what situations.

Ed Rutledge, one of the assistant coaches, scouted the Jets for us. Of course, we didn't know who our opponent was going to be until the results of the AFL championship game was in. Rutledge went to the game and took notes on both the Jets and the Oakland Raiders. He observed, for instance, what happened to players who went off the field with injuries, how they were treated on the sidelines. He watched the pre-game warm-ups; sometimes these give a clue as to which players aren't in topflight shape.

How do you assess the skills of Joe Namath?

Aside from the Super Bowl, I've only watched Namath on television, where I've seen him three or four times.

209

He has a fast release and sets up quickly. Even though he back pedals a bit deeper than most NFL quarterbacks, and has bad knees and can't do much scrambling, he doesn't get caught very often. This is because he has such a quick release.

Namath had a terrific day against us in Miami. He mixed his passes and running plays intelligently and really moved his team. He beat our blitz several times. And you can't criticize a quarterback who completes seventeen of twenty-eight passes. Everything he did worked. I'm sure if would be different if we were to play again.

Were either you or the Colts psyched by Joe Namath's pre-game remarks?

About a week before the Super Bowl game, Namath told an interviewer that he believed that American League quarterbacks were superior to National League quarterbacks, and that Daryle Lamonica did a better job at quarterback than I did. And he said Babe Parilli, the Jets back-up man, was a better passer, and that he, Namath, and John Hadl of the San Diego Chargers, and Bob Griese of the Miami Dolphins were all better. These remarks gained Joe a great deal of newspaper space—and I think that's exactly what he wanted. He obviously seems to thrive on being in the limelight; he relishes publicity.

Any player, not necessarily a quarterback, on any team, has information and opinions that would arch the eyebrows of most newspapermen, information that is worth reams of newspaper space. But players keep this news to themselves. At least, that's the way it's been traditionally. Maybe Namath represents the "new breed" of athlete, what the coming generation wants. But I hope not.

When you play football as long as I have, you eventually come up against virtually every type of individual, from the quiet introvert whose name appears only on the program book, to the swinger and the loudmouth, the player who will say anything to get his name in print. Neither characteristic has any effect on what happens on the field.

Do you feel that the outcome of the Super Bowl game might have been different if you hadn't done so well against Cleveland in the NFL championship game? In other words were you complacent about the Jets?

The fact that we had beaten the Browns, 34–0, was only one factor. We were rated as eighteen-point favorites before the Super Bowl, and I think this also could have worked to make us over-confident—but it didn't. I didn't detect any complacency. We respected the Jets. We knew we were going to have to go out and earn a victory. We were ready; we were "up."

Do you think the Colt's defense let the team down?

I think our defense played good football. They held the Jets to one touchdown and two field goals. The other field goal came about as the result of an offensive team letdown, a fumble.

I know many people were critical of the defense and singled out the right side of the line for special blame for not containing Matt Snell. But I'll take players like Fred Miller and Ordell Braase anytime in any situation. I can't fault them.

You have to give Matt Snell a good deal of credit. He gained 121 yards against us, mainly by picking the right hole and hitting it quick. Sometimes he'd start outside, but if he saw just a crack of daylight inside, he'd veer back in. He didn't make one wrong decision all day as far as I can recall.

Why didn't the Colts' front four get to Namath more often?

We began to blitz in the second period, with Rick Volk or Jerry Logan, our safeties, combining with linebackers Dennis Baubatz or Mike Curtis. According to Shula, Namath beat them. He simply unloaded the ball—usually to Sauer—before our men could get to him.

There were two other factors—Matt Snell's success in getting yardage on the ground, and our inability to score. The front four and the linebackers had to keep alert for Snell; they didn't want to give up any long yardage. And because we couldn't get points on the board, our defense had to play a more conservative game than usual. There is always an element of recklessness in the blitz, and as the afternoon wore on, the defense couldn't afford to be reckless; in fact, they had to become more cautious.

Why didn't you see Jimmy Orr in the end zone on the final play of the first half?

I should have seen him. Countless people have told me he was wide open. But I had to turn to the right in order to take the pass from Matte, and when I looked up, Jimmy wasn't in my line of vision. Jerry Hill was, and I went to him.

Why didn't the Colts go for a field goal on fourth and five on the Jets 19 with less than three minutes remaining and the Jets ahead, 16-7?

We needed a touchdown and a field goal to win. Shula decided to go for the touchdown because he didn't want to lose the field position the team had. If he had elected to go for the field goal and we had made it, we still would have had to be successful with another onside kickoff.

Do you feel the game's outcome would have been any different if you had stayed in, if Shula hadn't inserted Unitas in the lineup?

I can't really say, of course. I know that throughout my career I've been successful countless times in come-from-behind situations. And Johnny has a really remarkable record in this regard. But it's a moot point whether I would have fared better or worse than Johnny did.

If you had to prepare for the game again, what would you do that would be different?

Our game plan was well thought out. Our defenses were sound. Everyone was ready. Any changes that I might suggest would be quite minor. We just didn't make the scoring plays; they did. That was the difference.

Do you think the outcome of the game would be any different if the two teams were to meet again?

Definitely.

CHAPTER THIRTY

What happened that gloomy Sunday in Miami is still deeply engraved in my memory. Now, almost three years later, I can still recall every play in detail.

I used to worry about it. I used to worry that people would remember me as the quarterback who lost a Super Bowl game his team was supposed to win. Then came January, 1971, and another Super Bowl game for the Colts and, incredibly, another chance for me. This time it turned out better, much better. I'm not saying that what happened in the 1971 Super Bowl, when we turned back the Dallas Cowboys for the title, wiped away all the bitter memories. It couldn't do that. The game with the Jets is in the books. Nothing can ever change it. But beating the Cowboys sure eased the pain, and I think that in years to come that when the name Earl Morrall happens to come up, people will think of him as a winner too.

We opened the 1970 season by taking a squeaker. Jim O'Brien, our rookie kicker from the University of Cincinnati, booted his third field goal of the game with less than a minute to play, and we managed to nose out the Chargers, 16–14. Unitas did the quarterbacking. We came home the next week to meet Kansas City. It was brutal; we were never in the game. I forget the final score but the Chiefs scored seventeen points in the first sixteen minutes and wound up leading 31–7 at the half. They scored in each of the last two periods, too.

After the game I couldn't help but think our stumbling start was sadly reminiscent of the year before, a season in which we finished a distant second to the Rams in the Coastal Division of the Western Conference. That season we didn't merely stumble at the start; we fell on our faces, losing our first two games. At mid-season we were 4–3 and the Rams hadn't lost. They went on to win eleven in a row, wrapping up the title in late November.

We ended up the year with an 8–5–1 record, which triggered a mountain of criticism. People said we were in a state of shock because of what the Jets did to us in the Super Bowl. They said the team was racked by dissension, that Shula and several players were feuding.

What the critics didn't say was that Bobby Boyd, who had retired, was sorely missed, nor did they mention that John Mackey was bothered by a bad knee all season long, and his backup, Tom Mitchell, had injury problems. And the critics seemed to overlook that Jerry Hill and Terry Cole were also hampered by injuries, which crippled our running game, and Lou Michaels never attained his usual kicking form.

Another thing. An 8-5-1 record isn't *that* bad. Sometimes I think the winning tradition that the Colts have established, and the team's soundness year in and year out, has spoiled the fans. Any season in which the team loses more than two or three games is considered a bust. I know more than a handful of coaches who would spend the off-season happily if they could just manage to compile an 8-5-1 record.

As for the matter of discord between Shula and some players, that was much overplayed. Some of the stories I read bordered on the fictional. Shula is by nature a fiery guy, tense and excitable during the game. When something goes wrong, he lets the guy responsible know about it. But that's not a sign of dissension. That's how Shula operates. You can't put a bad rap on Shula. Just look at his coaching record.

After Shula defected to Miami, and Don McCafferty, our offensive backfield coach took over, I was a bit apprehensive. I thought the easy-going, sweet-tempered McCafferty might be too lenient, and that some of the guys would take advantage of him. But it never happened. McCafferty held the team in firm control all the way. The methods he used were different than Shula's however. Whereas Shula might scream at a player for making a mistake, McCafferty would have a private chat with him. And whereas Shula kept a lot of players in doubt as to where they stood, McCafferty operated with greater candor.

Our second game of the season, the one we lost to the Chiefs, is a case in point. Sure, McCafferty was upset after the game, and visibly so, especially since we had been beaten so convincingly. But he realized it was a game in which the Chiefs could do absolutely nothing wrong.

No one was openly critized. He told us what he expected of us in the future. And that was that.

That game was the season's low point for us. The next Sunday, with the players responding to McCafferty's gentle approach, we beat Boston, though it was close, 14–6, and, the following week, Houston, on a long touchdown pass play in the final seconds. This seemed to be the style of the 1970 Colts, winning the close ones in the last seconds. Then came a key game against the Jets. You remember the Jets.

It was a particularly important game because under the terms of the merger agreement that had been hammered out a couple of years before, we were now members of the American Conference of the Eastern Division. The Jets, Dolphins, Bills and Patriots were the other teams. We and the Jets were considered the strongest teams, and so our two scheduled meetings that season were considered vital to each of us.

The game was to be played at Shea Stadium and during the week we prepared for it no one made any speeches or gave any pep talks on how this was our chance to get some revenge for what happened in the Super Bowl. But on the Saturday morning before we left for New York, McCafferty had a team meeting at Memorial Stadium, and without saying a word he ran off the film of the Super Bowl game. He didn't stop the film to make any comments. He didn't say anything after, and neither did anyone else.

Did the strategy work? On the first play of the game, Unitas hit Mackey on a sideline pattern that got us 48 yards and set up a field goal. The next time we got the ball we scored a touchdown. It took us two-and-a-half minutes to put seventeen points on the board. The Jets never had a chance. Incidentally, this was the game in which Billy Ray Smith fell on Joe Namath, and Namath sustained a broken wrist which kept him on the sidelines for the rest of the season.

After we whipped the Jets, we kept right on rolling, winning four straight. This gave us a 7–1 record and a comfortable lead over the second place Dolphins, who were 4–4.

We then lost one and tied another, but if there were any doubts we weren't going to win the Division title, Unitas settled them in a game against Chicago late in the season. It was the type of performance for which Johnny is noted. The Bears jumped off to a big lead, scoring seventeen points in the first ten plays, by intercepting three of the first six passes Johnny threw.

But Johnny hung in there, even though he had two more passes stolen. In the game's closing minutes, we were behind by six points, when Johnny went back to throw once more. Eddie Hinton was his primary target. But as Johnny went back, he spotted a slip-up in the Chicago secondary. Both cornerbacks and safeties were rolling toward the outside, leaving the middle open, and John Mackey was there. Instantly Unitas read what was happening and whipped the ball to Mackey for a game-tieing touchdown. O'Brien booted the extra point to give us a 21–20 win.

There's one other game that stands out in my memory that season, the final game, a second meeting with the Jets. We had already clinched the championship, so the game was just a tune-up for the playoffs. But I'll never forget it.

I hadn't played much during the season. In fact, I had started only once and passed the ball only sixty times.

Johnny opened the Jet game at quarterback, but McCafferty put me in to replace him later in the first quarter. We were behind at the time, 7–0. We were using Roy Jefferson, normally a wide receiver, as a man in motion out of a tight T backfield. This was to get Jefferson free of the Jet defensemen, who liked to play bump and run.

The Jet secondary came apart. I connected with Eddie Hinton for a pair of touchdown passes during the second quarter, earning us a tie at halftime. In the third quarter, Jimmy Orr got loose behind Cecil Leonard, and I got the ball to him for a third touchdown. That wasn't the end of it. In the final quarter, Ray Perkins worked himself loose behind the other Jet cornerback, Steve Tannen, and that was another touchdown.

The four touchdown throws, plus the 348 yards my passes produced (eighteen completions in thirty-three attempts) were new personal highs, and I must say the game was something of a record-setter for me from an emotional standpoint, too. It wasn't that I considered it any kind of an atonement for the Super Bowl defeat. It was something else. Throughout the season, I had felt in top-flight condition. I knew I was ready. I knew that if I played I would do well. The Jet game proved this. It proved I could contribute during the playoffs or whatever might lie beyond.

Johnny was masterful in the playoffs, steering us past the Cincinnati Bengals and then the Oakland Raiders and into the Super Bowl. Miami and the Orange Bowl were to be the scene again. I was somewhat dejected as the day of the game drew near. I figured that I was going to be a spectator, that I wasn't going to get a chance to play unless things went badly for us or we managed to get way ahead.

Of course, I didn't figure on Johnny getting hurt. But late in the second quarter, pedaling back to pass, Johnny was tackled by defensive end George Andrie, at six-foot-six, and 250 pounds, a huge mountain of a man. Andrie's helmet and shoulder pads whacked Johnny in the ribs. Nothing was broken, but the pain was so great Johnny had to come out. Suddenly the whole thing was in my lap, I didn't think about what had happened before. I didn't have a chance to. My mind was filled with formations and plays we could use to beat the Dallas defenses.

After a Dallas punt, I went in. About three minutes were left in the half. I called a pass on the first play because I figured the Cowboys wouldn't be expecting it. And they weren't. Eddie Hinton got open and I whipped the ball to him for a twenty-six yard gain. It gave the team a lift. You could feel it.

Up to this point, very little had worked for us. We were down 13–6, and our only touchdown had come when one of Johnny's passes was tipped by Eddie Hinton, then by Mel Renfro of the Cowboys, and finally wound up in John Mackey's hands. John streaked into the end zone.

Now it was first down on the Cowboy 23. Time was running out in the half. I called a pass to Roy Jefferson. It got us twenty-one yards and first down on the Dallas 2. The clock was running, close to two minutes were left, plenty of time to get some points.

On first down I called a halfback slant, handing off to rookie Norm Bulaich, who hit the left side behind the blocking of fullback Tom Nowatzke. Bulaich had a good reputation for running over people, but the Cowboys clogged up the middle and Bulaich got nothing.

Because the Cowboys were jamming up the middle so well, I decided to send Bulaich around an end to get the two yards we needed. Nowatzke and Mackey would block. I handed to Bulaich and watched him pound to the right, then make his turn, and I saw middle linebacker Lee Roy Jordan move with him. All Bulaich had to do was cut back, cut to his left, and knife his way past Jordan. But instead Norm put his head down and tried to bowl over Jordan. That's what the Dallas veteran was hoping for, I guess, because he slammed into Bulaich, hitting him low, very low, and driving him back as he struck.

I called the play again. "Cut back," I told Bulaich. "Don't try to run over that guy." But this time Bulaich never got to the outside and when he tried the middle he was stopped dead. Three plays and we had gotten nothing —no yards, no points.

On our last try I decided to go to the air, calling a play that's listed as "119 weakside end delay" in the Colt playbook, a pass with Tom Mitchell as the primary receiver. Mitchell threw a block at linebacker Chuck Howley, but as he tried to slide off, Howley stayed with him. Mitchell, in trying to struggle free, got his feet tangled with tackle Jethro Pugh's and half stumbled. The Dallas front four was pressing me now and I had to throw. I purposely lofted the ball to give Mitchell an extra second to regain his momentum, but he never did. The pass went incomplete.

Dallas ran one play and the quarter ended. As I went off the field, I got a sickening flashback of our first Super Bowl game, a sort of taped replay of the last minute or so of the first half of that game. We hadn't scored then. We hadn't scored now. I figured I was in for a lot of sleepless nights during the coming year.

The third quarter was scoreless. Then midway on the final period, safety Rick Volk intercepted one of Craig Morton's passes on the Dallas 33 raced to the 3 before they brought him down. On second down, Tom Nowatzke hammered his way into the end zone. When O'Brien booted the extra point the score was tied.

For a while it looked like there was going to be a suddendeath overtime. But with about a minute left to play, Morton went back to pass to Dan Reeves. Our Jerry Logan slammed into Reeves as he moved to make the grab, and the ball popped into the hands of linebacker Mike Curtis. Mike got to the Dallas 28 before he was stopped.

218

We ran two running plays that got us three yards and then I called a timeout. There were nine seconds left, just enough time to boot a field goal. At the sidelines McCafferty grabbed me. "Talk to him, Earl" he said, motioning toward Jim O'Brien. "Keep him calm."

O'Brien was in a frenzy. "Let's go, Earl," he said. "Let's get out there."

"O'Bie," I said, "we've got plenty of time."

"Which way's the wind?"

"There's no wind."

"Should I kick it to the left post or the right?"

"Just boot it hard and down the middle."

As we lined up and I knelt to hold the ball, the Cowboys started screaming and yelling to rattle O'Brien. "He's going to choke," one guy was shouting. "He's going to miss," yelled another. Then another guy called a timeout. But they didn't have any timeouts left. They were only trying to unsettle poor O'Brien.

"Let's go! Let's go!," O'Brien shouted. "Put the ball down!"

It was wild. The Cowboys were yelling at him, and the officials were trying to get the game back on the track. Kneeling there, I turned to O'Brien. "We're O.K., O'Bie," I said. "There's plenty of time."

Finally we were ready to go again. Tom Goode was the center. I watched him grip the ball. I watched it right into my hands. I put it down. O'Brien's foot boomed through. I could tell by the sound that it was a solid hit. I lifted my head to watch. I swear my heart had stopped beating. It was no hard end-over-end kick; it kind of sailed, traveling a crazy path, first heading for the right post, but then looping back toward the middle to clear the bar by several feet.

I was frozen. I couldn't move. I just knelt there for a second or two. Then I saw O'Brien jumping up and down and the realization of what had happened hit me. We had won. We had won the Super Bowl. I leaped into the air. The newspapers had pictures of it. I was very high off the ground. Then came the celebrating in the dressing room. It was like a dream. I kept hoping I wasn't going to wake up.

Some people say my experience in the 1971 Super Bowl suggests great irony, or that it represents sweet atonement, or at least poetic justice. I guess any one or all of these could apply. But there's really no way to explain it. My wife says it's like the ending of a fairy tale. It is—but it's more. Someone upstairs played a big part in 'it.

There's one other question that needs to be asked: "What's ahead for Earl Morrall?"

Pro football players—indeed, athletes in general—are much more concerned about their futures nowadays than they were when I broke in with the Forty-Niners back in 1956, a time when a guy would be satisfied with an off-season job paying $125 a week as a public relations man for a beer company. Those days have gone the way of the single wing. Today's players are looking for solid career opportunities and equity situations.

It used to be that some players would spend the off-season working on construction jobs. Others went to the local gym and simply played basketball for the winter. I knew guys who spent the period from January to June staying at home watching their kids while their wives went out and worked. These players were in deep difficulty when their football careers ended. They were thirty-two to thirty-six years old and they had to go out and compete with guys twenty-one or twenty-two and just out of college, and most companies preferred the younger men. Even when a football veteran did land a job, he often found that he was paid at a trainee's rate or that of a beginner. He was several years behind his contemporaries. This made the transition period very rough.

When I arrived in Detroit in 1958, I noticed that many of my teammates held down good-paying sales jobs in the auto industry, working either for a major manufacturer or one of the hundreds of industry suppliers. They'd work full-time from January to June, then, once football season began, merely keep up their contacts until the season ended. That's what I've been doing for the past ten years or so. And I intend to remain in sales work, in a job that's related to the auto industry, when my playing days are over. In fact, in 1969, in partnership with Sonny Gandee, I opened a sales agency which represents companies that make parts for the automotive industry. The name of the firm is Earl Morrall Associates. We represent such companies as Aetna Stamping and Metal Forming, Falls Stamping and Welding, and Imerman Screw Products.

I never have had any strong desire to coach, especially

220

for a college. If the job involved only coaching per se, that is, the training and schooling of young players, I might feel differently. I enjoy working with youngsters. I coached Little League baseball when we lived in Pittsburgh and later in Detroit. Boys of eight, nine, and ten have such a keen interest in the game and their skills develop so rapidly that coaching them is a rewarding experience. But coaching for a college involves an enormous amount of scouting and recruiting during the off-season. Moreover, coaches are usually hired on a year-to-year basis, and this situation hardly appeals to me.

Pro football has proved to be a big asset in the sales work I do. It provides an entree; I'm able to get to see people I never would otherwise. This is especially true nowadays with pro football more popular than ever before. People want to talk about it, to gain some insight into the sport.

Of course, being a pro quarterback only provides the opportunity. You still have to make the calls; you still have to do the selling.

I have a boy who will be starting college in a few years, and I hope he'll be interested in sports, not necessarily football, but any one of the major sports. A career in football, baseball, or basketball can be a steppingstone to a career in the business world, but that's only part of it.

I believe that sports help to build a boy's courage and confidence. They teach self-discipline and the value of hard work. They teach a boy how to accept adversity.

Sports have helped me to meet people and to enjoy them. I'm no Jackie Gleason; I'm not even an Alex Karras, but I can address a group of almost any size with ease and confidence.

I don't say I got more out of football than I did out of the classroom. The two go hand in hand. In time, your athletic skills diminish, but you retain your academic training forever.

Ever since my eighth or ninth year in professional football, people have been asking me how much longer I expect to be playing. You never really know. You can never plan. You can be headed for the greatest season of your career, then all of a sudden you're hit by an injury and everything becomes a shambles. You're through. I've seen it happen time after time. I thought it might have happened to me after I broke my wrist in 1966.

What I'm saying is that you learn to take one year at a time. You learn to count on nothing, even if you're the NFL Player of the Year.

More and more I'm beginning to wonder what it will be like when I'm not playing football. It will be a jolt, I know. I've played through high school, college, and counting the 1970 season, for fifteen years in the pros. That's twenty-two years in all, more than half my lifetime.

I'll miss a lot. I'll miss the whole idea of football, the physical part, just being in uniform and stepping out on to the field, even if it's just a practice, and throwing and working out. I really enjoy that.

I'll miss the games and the tremendous exhilaration you get from them. I guess I'll even miss the tension.

But most of all I'll miss being a part of the team, the closeness and the friendships you build up over the years. I know what it's like to sit on the bench. I remember when I broke my wrist and had to sit out half the season. I just didn't feel a part of the team any more.

That's what I'll miss the most—that closeness. I hate to give it up.

EARL MORRALL CAREER PASSING RECORD

Year	Team	Games	At-tempts	Comple-tions	Pct. Comp.	Yards	Tds.	Int.	Average Gain
1956	San Francisco	12	78	38	48.7	621	1	6	7.96
1957	Pittsburgh	12	289	139	48.1	1900	11	12	6.57
1958	Pitts-Det	11	78	25	32.1	463	5	9	5.94
1959	Detroit	12	137	65	47.4	1102	5	6	8.04
1960	Detroit	12	49	32	65.3	423	4	3	8.63
1961	Detroit	13	150	69	46.0	909	7	9	6.06
1962	Detroit	14	52	32	61.5	449	4	4	8.63
1963	Detroit	14	328	174	53.0	2621	24	14	7.99
1964	Detroit	6	91	50	54.9	588	4	3	6.46
1965	New York	14	302	155	51.3	2446	22	12	8.10
1966	New York	7	151	71	47.0	1105	7	12	7.32
1967	New York	8	24	13	54.2	181	3	1	7.54
1968	Baltimore	14	317	182	57.4	2909	26	17	9.18
1969	Baltimore	14	99	46	46.5	755	5	7	7.63
1970	Baltimore	14	93	51	54.8	792	9	4	8.52
1971	Baltimore	12	167	84	50.3	1210	7	13	14.7

EARL MORRALL CAREER RUSHING RECORD

Year	Team	Attempts	Yards	Average	Touchdowns
1956	San Francisco	6	10	1.7	0
1957	Pittsburgh	41	81	2.0	2
1958	Pitts-Det.	11	80	7.3	0
1959	Detroit	26	112	4.3	0
1960	Detroit	10	37	3.7	1
1961	Detroit	20	86	4.3	0
1962	Detroit	17	65	3.8	1
1963	Detroit	26	105	4.0	1
1964	Detroit	10	70	7.0	0
1965	New York	17	52	3.1	0
1966	New York	5	12	2.4	0
1967	New York	4	11	2.8	1
1968	Baltimore	11	18	1.6	1
1969	Baltimore	0	0	0	0
1970	Baltimore	2	6	3.0	0
1971	Baltimore	no carries			

EARL MORRALL CAREER PUNTING RECORD

Year	Team	Games	Number	Average Distance	Blocked
1956	San Francisco	12	45	37.9	0
1958	Pitts-Det.	11	1	25.0	0
1959	Detroit	12	11	43.7	0
1961	Detroit	13	3	37.7	0
1962	Detroit	14	1	48.0	0
1963	Detroit	14	29	39.4	0
1964	Detroit	6	1	8.0	0
1967	New York	8	15	31.5	1